C-94   **CAREER EXAMINATION SERIES**

*This is your
PASSBOOK for...*

Bridge & Tunnel Maintainer

*Test Preparation Study Guide
Questions & Answers*

COPYRIGHT NOTICE

This book is SOLELY intended for, is sold ONLY to, and its use is RESTRICTED to individual, bona fide applicants or candidates who qualify by virtue of having seriously filed applications for appropriate license, certificate, professional and/or promotional advancement, higher school matriculation, scholarship, or other legitimate requirements of education and/or governmental authorities.

This book is NOT intended for use, class instruction, tutoring, training, duplication, copying, reprinting, excerption, or adaptation, etc., by:

1) Other publishers
2) Proprietors and/or Instructors of "Coaching" and/or Preparatory Courses
3) Personnel and/or Training Divisions of commercial, industrial, and governmental organizations
4) Schools, colleges, or universities and/or their departments and staffs, including teachers and other personnel
5) Testing Agencies or Bureaus
6) Study groups which seek by the purchase of a single volume to copy and/or duplicate and/or adapt this material for use by the group as a whole without having purchased individual volumes for each of the members of the group
7) Et al.

Such persons would be in violation of appropriate Federal and State statutes.

PROVISION OF LICENSING AGREEMENTS – Recognized educational, commercial, industrial, and governmental institutions and organizations, and others legitimately engaged in educational pursuits, including training, testing, and measurement activities, may address request for a licensing agreement to the copyright owners, who will determine whether, and under what conditions, including fees and charges, the materials in this book may be used them. In other words, a licensing facility exists for the legitimate use of the material in this book on other than an individual basis. However, it is asseverated and affirmed here that the material in this book CANNOT be used without the receipt of the express permission of such a licensing agreement from the Publishers. Inquiries re licensing should be addressed to the company, attention rights and permissions department.

All rights reserved, including the right of reproduction in whole or in part, in any form or by any means, electronic or mechanical, including photocopying, recording, or by any information storage and retrieval system, without permission in writing from the Publisher.

Copyright © 2024 by
National Learning Corporation

212 Michael Drive, Syosset, NY 11791
(516) 921-8888 • www.passbooks.com
E-mail: info@passbooks.com

PASSBOOK® SERIES

THE *PASSBOOK® SERIES* has been created to prepare applicants and candidates for the ultimate academic battlefield – the examination room.

At some time in our lives, each and every one of us may be required to take an examination – for validation, matriculation, admission, qualification, registration, certification, or licensure.

Based on the assumption that every applicant or candidate has met the basic formal educational standards, has taken the required number of courses, and read the necessary texts, the *PASSBOOK® SERIES* furnishes the one special preparation which may assure passing with confidence, instead of failing with insecurity. Examination questions – together with answers – are furnished as the basic vehicle for study so that the mysteries of the examination and its compounding difficulties may be eliminated or diminished by a sure method.

This book is meant to help you pass your examination provided that you qualify and are serious in your objective.

The entire field is reviewed through the huge store of content information which is succinctly presented through a provocative and challenging approach – the question-and-answer method.

A climate of success is established by furnishing the correct answers at the end of each test.

You soon learn to recognize types of questions, forms of questions, and patterns of questioning. You may even begin to anticipate expected outcomes.

You perceive that many questions are repeated or adapted so that you can gain acute insights, which may enable you to score many sure points.

You learn how to confront new questions, or types of questions, and to attack them confidently and work out the correct answers.

You note objectives and emphases, and recognize pitfalls and dangers, so that you may make positive educational adjustments.

Moreover, you are kept fully informed in relation to new concepts, methods, practices, and directions in the field.

You discover that you are actually taking the examination all the time: you are preparing for the examination by "taking" an examination, not by reading extraneous and/or supererogatory textbooks.

In short, this PASSBOOK®, used directedly, should be an important factor in helping you to pass your test.

BRIDGE AND TUNNEL MAINTAINER

DUTIES AND RESPONSIBILITIES

Under general supervision, maintains and operates the varied facilities and equipment of the bridge and tunnel authority. Performs related work.

EXAMPLES OF TYPICAL TASKS

Maintains buildings, fixed bridges, tunnels and parts of the foregoing structures. Climbs bridge structures and main suspension cables and performs work on same. Maintains and operates movable bridges. Maintains and repairs electrical wiring systems, power and control equipment, and automotive and mechanical equipment. Paints and installs signs. Uses and maintains shops required for the continued operation of the authority's facilities. May supervise employees maintaining and operating facilities and equipment and performing related work. Drives vehicles when required by the work assignment. Clears snow, removes debris, and cleans the authority facilities.

TESTS

The written test will be of the multiple-choice type and may contain questions designed to test for fundamental electrical principles and the ability to maintain and repair electrical wiring, controls and equipment; fundamental automotive mechanics and mechanical principles and the ability to maintain and repair vehicles and other mechanical equipment; operation of mechanical equipment used to clear snow, remove debris and clean bridge and tunnel authority facilities; correct and safe use of tools and the elements of good workmanship in the maintenance and repair of electrical and mechanical equipment; fabrication and installation of signs and proper painting techniques; techniques for arc-welding, carpentry and plumbing; elementary knowledge of supervision; and other related areas.

HOW TO TAKE A TEST

I. YOU MUST PASS AN EXAMINATION

A. *WHAT EVERY CANDIDATE SHOULD KNOW*

Examination applicants often ask us for help in preparing for the written test. What can I study in advance? What kinds of questions will be asked? How will the test be given? How will the papers be graded?

As an applicant for a civil service examination, you may be wondering about some of these things. Our purpose here is to suggest effective methods of advance study and to describe civil service examinations.

Your chances for success on this examination can be increased if you know how to prepare. Those "pre-examination jitters" can be reduced if you know what to expect. You can even experience an adventure in good citizenship if you know why civil service exams are given.

B. *WHY ARE CIVIL SERVICE EXAMINATIONS GIVEN?*

Civil service examinations are important to you in two ways. As a citizen, you want public jobs filled by employees who know how to do their work. As a job seeker, you want a fair chance to compete for that job on an equal footing with other candidates. The best-known means of accomplishing this two-fold goal is the competitive examination.

Exams are widely publicized throughout the nation. They may be administered for jobs in federal, state, city, municipal, town or village governments or agencies.

Any citizen may apply, with some limitations, such as the age or residence of applicants. Your experience and education may be reviewed to see whether you meet the requirements for the particular examination. When these requirements exist, they are reasonable and applied consistently to all applicants. Thus, a competitive examination may cause you some uneasiness now, but it is your privilege and safeguard.

C. *HOW ARE CIVIL SERVICE EXAMS DEVELOPED?*

Examinations are carefully written by trained technicians who are specialists in the field known as "psychological measurement," in consultation with recognized authorities in the field of work that the test will cover. These experts recommend the subject matter areas or skills to be tested; only those knowledges or skills important to your success on the job are included. The most reliable books and source materials available are used as references. Together, the experts and technicians judge the difficulty level of the questions.

Test technicians know how to phrase questions so that the problem is clearly stated. Their ethics do not permit "trick" or "catch" questions. Questions may have been tried out on sample groups, or subjected to statistical analysis, to determine their usefulness.

Written tests are often used in combination with performance tests, ratings of training and experience, and oral interviews. All of these measures combine to form the best-known means of finding the right person for the right job.

II. HOW TO PASS THE WRITTEN TEST

A. NATURE OF THE EXAMINATION

To prepare intelligently for civil service examinations, you should know how they differ from school examinations you have taken. In school you were assigned certain definite pages to read or subjects to cover. The examination questions were quite detailed and usually emphasized memory. Civil service exams, on the other hand, try to discover your present ability to perform the duties of a position, plus your potentiality to learn these duties. In other words, a civil service exam attempts to predict how successful you will be. Questions cover such a broad area that they cannot be as minute and detailed as school exam questions.

In the public service similar kinds of work, or positions, are grouped together in one "class." This process is known as *position-classification*. All the positions in a class are paid according to the salary range for that class. One class title covers all of these positions, and they are all tested by the same examination.

B. FOUR BASIC STEPS

1) Study the announcement

How, then, can you know what subjects to study? Our best answer is: "Learn as much as possible about the class of positions for which you've applied." The exam will test the knowledge, skills and abilities needed to do the work.

Your most valuable source of information about the position you want is the official exam announcement. This announcement lists the training and experience qualifications. Check these standards and apply only if you come reasonably close to meeting them.

The brief description of the position in the examination announcement offers some clues to the subjects which will be tested. Think about the job itself. Review the duties in your mind. Can you perform them, or are there some in which you are rusty? Fill in the blank spots in your preparation.

Many jurisdictions preview the written test in the exam announcement by including a section called "Knowledge and Abilities Required," "Scope of the Examination," or some similar heading. Here you will find out specifically what fields will be tested.

2) Review your own background

Once you learn in general what the position is all about, and what you need to know to do the work, ask yourself which subjects you already know fairly well and which need improvement. You may wonder whether to concentrate on improving your strong areas or on building some background in your fields of weakness. When the announcement has specified "some knowledge" or "considerable knowledge," or has used adjectives like "beginning principles of..." or "advanced ... methods," you can get a clue as to the number and difficulty of questions to be asked in any given field. More questions, and hence broader coverage, would be included for those subjects which are more important in the work. Now weigh your strengths and weaknesses against the job requirements and prepare accordingly.

3) Determine the level of the position

Another way to tell how intensively you should prepare is to understand the level of the job for which you are applying. Is it the entering level? In other words, is this the position in which beginners in a field of work are hired? Or is it an intermediate or advanced level? Sometimes this is indicated by such words as "Junior" or "Senior" in the class title. Other jurisdictions use Roman numerals to designate the level – Clerk I, Clerk II, for example. The word "Supervisor" sometimes appears in the title. If the level is not indicated by the title, check the description of duties. Will you be working under very close supervision, or will you have responsibility for independent decisions in this work?

4) Choose appropriate study materials

Now that you know the subjects to be examined and the relative amount of each subject to be covered, you can choose suitable study materials. For beginning level jobs, or even advanced ones, if you have a pronounced weakness in some aspect of your training, read a modern, standard textbook in that field. Be sure it is up to date and has general coverage. Such books are normally available at your library, and the librarian will be glad to help you locate one. For entry-level positions, questions of appropriate difficulty are chosen – neither highly advanced questions, nor those too simple. Such questions require careful thought but not advanced training.

If the position for which you are applying is technical or advanced, you will read more advanced, specialized material. If you are already familiar with the basic principles of your field, elementary textbooks would waste your time. Concentrate on advanced textbooks and technical periodicals. Think through the concepts and review difficult problems in your field.

These are all general sources. You can get more ideas on your own initiative, following these leads. For example, training manuals and publications of the government agency which employs workers in your field can be useful, particularly for technical and professional positions. A letter or visit to the government department involved may result in more specific study suggestions, and certainly will provide you with a more definite idea of the exact nature of the position you are seeking.

III. KINDS OF TESTS

Tests are used for purposes other than measuring knowledge and ability to perform specified duties. For some positions, it is equally important to test ability to make adjustments to new situations or to profit from training. In others, basic mental abilities not dependent on information are essential. Questions which test these things may not appear as pertinent to the duties of the position as those which test for knowledge and information. Yet they are often highly important parts of a fair examination. For very general questions, it is almost impossible to help you direct your study efforts. What we can do is to point out some of the more common of these general abilities needed in public service positions and describe some typical questions.

1) General information

Broad, general information has been found useful for predicting job success in some kinds of work. This is tested in a variety of ways, from vocabulary lists to questions about current events. Basic background in some field of work, such as sociology or economics, may be sampled in a group of questions. Often these are principles which have become familiar to most persons through exposure rather than through formal training. It is difficult to advise you how to study for these questions; being alert to the world around you is our best suggestion.

2) Verbal ability

An example of an ability needed in many positions is verbal or language ability. Verbal ability is, in brief, the ability to use and understand words. Vocabulary and grammar tests are typical measures of this ability. Reading comprehension or paragraph interpretation questions are common in many kinds of civil service tests. You are given a paragraph of written material and asked to find its central meaning.

3) Numerical ability

Number skills can be tested by the familiar arithmetic problem, by checking paired lists of numbers to see which are alike and which are different, or by interpreting charts and graphs. In the latter test, a graph may be printed in the test booklet which you are asked to use as the basis for answering questions.

4) Observation

A popular test for law-enforcement positions is the observation test. A picture is shown to you for several minutes, then taken away. Questions about the picture test your ability to observe both details and larger elements.

5) Following directions

In many positions in the public service, the employee must be able to carry out written instructions dependably and accurately. You may be given a chart with several columns, each column listing a variety of information. The questions require you to carry out directions involving the information given in the chart.

6) Skills and aptitudes

Performance tests effectively measure some manual skills and aptitudes. When the skill is one in which you are trained, such as typing or shorthand, you can practice. These tests are often very much like those given in business school or high school courses. For many of the other skills and aptitudes, however, no short-time preparation can be made. Skills and abilities natural to you or that you have developed throughout your lifetime are being tested.

Many of the general questions just described provide all the data needed to answer the questions and ask you to use your reasoning ability to find the answers. Your best preparation for these tests, as well as for tests of facts and ideas, is to be at your physical and mental best. You, no doubt, have your own methods of getting into an exam-taking mood and keeping "in shape." The next section lists some ideas on this subject.

IV. KINDS OF QUESTIONS

Only rarely is the "essay" question, which you answer in narrative form, used in civil service tests. Civil service tests are usually of the short-answer type. Full instructions for answering these questions will be given to you at the examination. But in case this is your first experience with short-answer questions and separate answer sheets, here is what you need to know:

1) Multiple-choice Questions

Most popular of the short-answer questions is the "multiple choice" or "best answer" question. It can be used, for example, to test for factual knowledge, ability to solve problems or judgment in meeting situations found at work.

A multiple-choice question is normally one of three types—
- It can begin with an incomplete statement followed by several possible endings. You are to find the one ending which *best* completes the statement, although some of the others may not be entirely wrong.
- It can also be a complete statement in the form of a question which is answered by choosing one of the statements listed.

- It can be in the form of a problem – again you select the best answer.

Here is an example of a multiple-choice question with a discussion which should give you some clues as to the method for choosing the right answer:

When an employee has a complaint about his assignment, the action which will *best* help him overcome his difficulty is to
   A. discuss his difficulty with his coworkers
   B. take the problem to the head of the organization
   C. take the problem to the person who gave him the assignment
   D. say nothing to anyone about his complaint

In answering this question, you should study each of the choices to find which is best. Consider choice "A" – Certainly an employee may discuss his complaint with fellow employees, but no change or improvement can result, and the complaint remains unresolved. Choice "B" is a poor choice since the head of the organization probably does not know what assignment you have been given, and taking your problem to him is known as "going over the head" of the supervisor. The supervisor, or person who made the assignment, is the person who can clarify it or correct any injustice. Choice "C" is, therefore, correct. To say nothing, as in choice "D," is unwise. Supervisors have and interest in knowing the problems employees are facing, and the employee is seeking a solution to his problem.

2) True/False Questions

The "true/false" or "right/wrong" form of question is sometimes used. Here a complete statement is given. Your job is to decide whether the statement is right or wrong.

SAMPLE: A roaming cell-phone call to a nearby city costs less than a non-roaming call to a distant city.

This statement is wrong, or false, since roaming calls are more expensive.

This is not a complete list of all possible question forms, although most of the others are variations of these common types. You will always get complete directions for answering questions. Be sure you understand *how* to mark your answers – ask questions until you do.

V. RECORDING YOUR ANSWERS

Computer terminals are used more and more today for many different kinds of exams.
For an examination with very few applicants, you may be told to record your answers in the test booklet itself. Separate answer sheets are much more common. If this separate answer sheet is to be scored by machine – and this is often the case – it is highly important that you mark your answers correctly in order to get credit.
An electronic scoring machine is often used in civil service offices because of the speed with which papers can be scored. Machine-scored answer sheets must be marked with a pencil, which will be given to you. This pencil has a high graphite content which responds to the electronic scoring machine. As a matter of fact, stray dots may register as answers, so do not let your pencil rest on the answer sheet while you are pondering the correct answer. Also, if your pencil lead breaks or is otherwise defective, ask for another.

Since the answer sheet will be dropped in a slot in the scoring machine, be careful not to bend the corners or get the paper crumpled.

The answer sheet normally has five vertical columns of numbers, with 30 numbers to a column. These numbers correspond to the question numbers in your test booklet. After each number, going across the page are four or five pairs of dotted lines. These short dotted lines have small letters or numbers above them. The first two pairs may also have a "T" or "F" above the letters. This indicates that the first two pairs only are to be used if the questions are of the true-false type. If the questions are multiple choice, disregard the "T" and "F" and pay attention only to the small letters or numbers.

Answer your questions in the manner of the sample that follows:

32. The largest city in the United States is
    A. Washington, D.C.
    B. New York City
    C. Chicago
    D. Detroit
    E. San Francisco

1) Choose the answer you think is best. (New York City is the largest, so "B" is correct.)
2) Find the row of dotted lines numbered the same as the question you are answering. (Find row number 32)
3) Find the pair of dotted lines corresponding to the answer. (Find the pair of lines under the mark "B.")
4) Make a solid black mark between the dotted lines.

VI. BEFORE THE TEST

Common sense will help you find procedures to follow to get ready for an examination. Too many of us, however, overlook these sensible measures. Indeed, nervousness and fatigue have been found to be the most serious reasons why applicants fail to do their best on civil service tests. Here is a list of reminders:

- Begin your preparation early – Don't wait until the last minute to go scurrying around for books and materials or to find out what the position is all about.
- Prepare continuously – An hour a night for a week is better than an all-night cram session. This has been definitely established. What is more, a night a week for a month will return better dividends than crowding your study into a shorter period of time.
- Locate the place of the exam – You have been sent a notice telling you when and where to report for the examination. If the location is in a different town or otherwise unfamiliar to you, it would be well to inquire the best route and learn something about the building.
- Relax the night before the test – Allow your mind to rest. Do not study at all that night. Plan some mild recreation or diversion; then go to bed early and get a good night's sleep.
- Get up early enough to make a leisurely trip to the place for the test – This way unforeseen events, traffic snarls, unfamiliar buildings, etc. will not upset you.
- Dress comfortably – A written test is not a fashion show. You will be known by number and not by name, so wear something comfortable.

- Leave excess paraphernalia at home – Shopping bags and odd bundles will get in your way. You need bring only the items mentioned in the official notice you received; usually everything you need is provided. Do not bring reference books to the exam. They will only confuse those last minutes and be taken away from you when in the test room.
- Arrive somewhat ahead of time – If because of transportation schedules you must get there very early, bring a newspaper or magazine to take your mind off yourself while waiting.
- Locate the examination room – When you have found the proper room, you will be directed to the seat or part of the room where you will sit. Sometimes you are given a sheet of instructions to read while you are waiting. Do not fill out any forms until you are told to do so; just read them and be prepared.
- Relax and prepare to listen to the instructions
- If you have any physical problem that may keep you from doing your best, be sure to tell the test administrator. If you are sick or in poor health, you really cannot do your best on the exam. You can come back and take the test some other time.

VII. AT THE TEST

The day of the test is here and you have the test booklet in your hand. The temptation to get going is very strong. Caution! There is more to success than knowing the right answers. You must know how to identify your papers and understand variations in the type of short-answer question used in this particular examination. Follow these suggestions for maximum results from your efforts:

1) Cooperate with the monitor

The test administrator has a duty to create a situation in which you can be as much at ease as possible. He will give instructions, tell you when to begin, check to see that you are marking your answer sheet correctly, and so on. He is not there to guard you, although he will see that your competitors do not take unfair advantage. He wants to help you do your best.

2) Listen to all instructions

Don't jump the gun! Wait until you understand all directions. In most civil service tests you get more time than you need to answer the questions. So don't be in a hurry. Read each word of instructions until you clearly understand the meaning. Study the examples, listen to all announcements and follow directions. Ask questions if you do not understand what to do.

3) Identify your papers

Civil service exams are usually identified by number only. You will be assigned a number; you must not put your name on your test papers. Be sure to copy your number correctly. Since more than one exam may be given, copy your exact examination title.

4) Plan your time

Unless you are told that a test is a "speed" or "rate of work" test, speed itself is usually not important. Time enough to answer all the questions will be provided, but this does not mean that you have all day. An overall time limit has been set. Divide the total time (in minutes) by the number of questions to determine the approximate time you have for each question.

5) Do not linger over difficult questions

If you come across a difficult question, mark it with a paper clip (useful to have along) and come back to it when you have been through the booklet. One caution if you do this – be sure to skip a number on your answer sheet as well. Check often to be sure that you have not lost your place and that you are marking in the row numbered the same as the question you are answering.

6) Read the questions

Be sure you know what the question asks! Many capable people are unsuccessful because they failed to *read* the questions correctly.

7) Answer all questions

Unless you have been instructed that a penalty will be deducted for incorrect answers, it is better to guess than to omit a question.

8) Speed tests

It is often better NOT to guess on speed tests. It has been found that on timed tests people are tempted to spend the last few seconds before time is called in marking answers at random – without even reading them – in the hope of picking up a few extra points. To discourage this practice, the instructions may warn you that your score will be "corrected" for guessing. That is, a penalty will be applied. The incorrect answers will be deducted from the correct ones, or some other penalty formula will be used.

9) Review your answers

If you finish before time is called, go back to the questions you guessed or omitted to give them further thought. Review other answers if you have time.

10) Return your test materials

If you are ready to leave before others have finished or time is called, take ALL your materials to the monitor and leave quietly. Never take any test material with you. The monitor can discover whose papers are not complete, and taking a test booklet may be grounds for disqualification.

VIII. EXAMINATION TECHNIQUES

1) Read the general instructions carefully. These are usually printed on the first page of the exam booklet. As a rule, these instructions refer to the timing of the examination; the fact that you should not start work until the signal and must stop work at a signal, etc. If there are any *special* instructions, such as a choice of questions to be answered, make sure that you note this instruction carefully.

2) When you are ready to start work on the examination, that is as soon as the signal has been given, read the instructions to each question booklet, underline any key words or phrases, such as *least, best, outline, describe* and the like. In this way you will tend to answer as requested rather than discover on reviewing your paper that you *listed without describing*, that you selected the *worst* choice rather than the *best* choice, etc.

3) If the examination is of the objective or multiple-choice type – that is, each question will also give a series of possible answers: A, B, C or D, and you are called upon to select the best answer and write the letter next to that answer on your answer paper – it is advisable to start answering each question in turn. There may be anywhere from 50 to 100 such questions in the three or four hours allotted and you can see how much time would be taken if you read through all the questions before beginning to answer any. Furthermore, if you come across a question or group of questions which you know would be difficult to answer, it would undoubtedly affect your handling of all the other questions.

4) If the examination is of the essay type and contains but a few questions, it is a moot point as to whether you should read all the questions before starting to answer any one. Of course, if you are given a choice – say five out of seven and the like – then it is essential to read all the questions so you can eliminate the two that are most difficult. If, however, you are asked to answer all the questions, there may be danger in trying to answer the easiest one first because you may find that you will spend too much time on it. The best technique is to answer the first question, then proceed to the second, etc.

5) Time your answers. Before the exam begins, write down the time it started, then add the time allowed for the examination and write down the time it must be completed, then divide the time available somewhat as follows:
    - If 3-1/2 hours are allowed, that would be 210 minutes. If you have 80 objective-type questions, that would be an average of 2-1/2 minutes per question. Allow yourself no more than 2 minutes per question, or a total of 160 minutes, which will permit about 50 minutes to review.
    - If for the time allotment of 210 minutes there are 7 essay questions to answer, that would average about 30 minutes a question. Give yourself only 25 minutes per question so that you have about 35 minutes to review.

6) The most important instruction is to *read each question* and make sure you know what is wanted. The second most important instruction is to *time yourself properly* so that you answer every question. The third most important instruction is to *answer every question*. Guess if you have to but include something for each question. Remember that you will receive no credit for a blank and will probably receive some credit if you write something in answer to an essay question. If you guess a letter – say "B" for a multiple-choice question – you may have guessed right. If you leave a blank as an answer to a multiple-choice question, the examiners may respect your feelings but it will not add a point to your score. Some exams may penalize you for wrong answers, so in such cases *only*, you may not want to guess unless you have some basis for your answer.

7) Suggestions
    a. Objective-type questions
        1. Examine the question booklet for proper sequence of pages and questions
        2. Read all instructions carefully
        3. Skip any question which seems too difficult; return to it after all other questions have been answered
        4. Apportion your time properly; do not spend too much time on any single question or group of questions

5. Note and underline key words – *all, most, fewest, least, best, worst, same, opposite*, etc.
6. Pay particular attention to negatives
7. Note unusual option, e.g., unduly long, short, complex, different or similar in content to the body of the question
8. Observe the use of "hedging" words – *probably, may, most likely*, etc.
9. Make sure that your answer is put next to the same number as the question
10. Do not second-guess unless you have good reason to believe the second answer is definitely more correct
11. Cross out original answer if you decide another answer is more accurate; do not erase until you are ready to hand your paper in
12. Answer all questions; guess unless instructed otherwise
13. Leave time for review

   b. Essay questions
     1. Read each question carefully
     2. Determine exactly what is wanted. Underline key words or phrases.
     3. Decide on outline or paragraph answer
     4. Include many different points and elements unless asked to develop any one or two points or elements
     5. Show impartiality by giving pros and cons unless directed to select one side only
     6. Make and write down any assumptions you find necessary to answer the questions
     7. Watch your English, grammar, punctuation and choice of words
     8. Time your answers; don't crowd material

8) Answering the essay question

Most essay questions can be answered by framing the specific response around several key words or ideas. Here are a few such key words or ideas:

M's: manpower, materials, methods, money, management
P's: purpose, program, policy, plan, procedure, practice, problems, pitfalls, personnel, public relations

   a. Six basic steps in handling problems:
     1. Preliminary plan and background development
     2. Collect information, data and facts
     3. Analyze and interpret information, data and facts
     4. Analyze and develop solutions as well as make recommendations
     5. Prepare report and sell recommendations
     6. Install recommendations and follow up effectiveness

   b. Pitfalls to avoid
     1. *Taking things for granted* – A statement of the situation does not necessarily imply that each of the elements is necessarily true; for example, a complaint may be invalid and biased so that all that can be taken for granted is that a complaint has been registered

2. *Considering only one side of a situation* – Wherever possible, indicate several alternatives and then point out the reasons you selected the best one
3. *Failing to indicate follow up* – Whenever your answer indicates action on your part, make certain that you will take proper follow-up action to see how successful your recommendations, procedures or actions turn out to be
4. *Taking too long in answering any single question* – Remember to time your answers properly

IX. AFTER THE TEST

Scoring procedures differ in detail among civil service jurisdictions although the general principles are the same. Whether the papers are hand-scored or graded by machine we have described, they are nearly always graded by number. That is, the person who marks the paper knows only the number – never the name – of the applicant. Not until all the papers have been graded will they be matched with names. If other tests, such as training and experience or oral interview ratings have been given, scores will be combined. Different parts of the examination usually have different weights. For example, the written test might count 60 percent of the final grade, and a rating of training and experience 40 percent. In many jurisdictions, veterans will have a certain number of points added to their grades.

After the final grade has been determined, the names are placed in grade order and an eligible list is established. There are various methods for resolving ties between those who get the same final grade – probably the most common is to place first the name of the person whose application was received first. Job offers are made from the eligible list in the order the names appear on it. You will be notified of your grade and your rank as soon as all these computations have been made. This will be done as rapidly as possible.

People who are found to meet the requirements in the announcement are called "eligibles." Their names are put on a list of eligible candidates. An eligible's chances of getting a job depend on how high he stands on this list and how fast agencies are filling jobs from the list.

When a job is to be filled from a list of eligibles, the agency asks for the names of people on the list of eligibles for that job. When the civil service commission receives this request, it sends to the agency the names of the three people highest on this list. Or, if the job to be filled has specialized requirements, the office sends the agency the names of the top three persons who meet these requirements from the general list.

The appointing officer makes a choice from among the three people whose names were sent to him. If the selected person accepts the appointment, the names of the others are put back on the list to be considered for future openings.

That is the rule in hiring from all kinds of eligible lists, whether they are for typist, carpenter, chemist, or something else. For every vacancy, the appointing officer has his choice of any one of the top three eligibles on the list. This explains why the person whose name is on top of the list sometimes does not get an appointment when some of the persons lower on the list do. If the appointing officer chooses the second or third eligible, the No. 1 eligible does not get a job at once, but stays on the list until he is appointed or the list is terminated.

X. HOW TO PASS THE INTERVIEW TEST

The examination for which you applied requires an oral interview test. You have already taken the written test and you are now being called for the interview test – the final part of the formal examination.

You may think that it is not possible to prepare for an interview test and that there are no procedures to follow during an interview. Our purpose is to point out some things you can do in advance that will help you and some good rules to follow and pitfalls to avoid while you are being interviewed.

What is an interview supposed to test?

The written examination is designed to test the technical knowledge and competence of the candidate; the oral is designed to evaluate intangible qualities, not readily measured otherwise, and to establish a list showing the relative fitness of each candidate – as measured against his competitors – for the position sought. Scoring is not on the basis of "right" and "wrong," but on a sliding scale of values ranging from "not passable" to "outstanding." As a matter of fact, it is possible to achieve a relatively low score without a single "incorrect" answer because of evident weakness in the qualities being measured.

Occasionally, an examination may consist entirely of an oral test – either an individual or a group oral. In such cases, information is sought concerning the technical knowledges and abilities of the candidate, since there has been no written examination for this purpose. More commonly, however, an oral test is used to supplement a written examination.

Who conducts interviews?

The composition of oral boards varies among different jurisdictions. In nearly all, a representative of the personnel department serves as chairman. One of the members of the board may be a representative of the department in which the candidate would work. In some cases, "outside experts" are used, and, frequently, a businessman or some other representative of the general public is asked to serve. Labor and management or other special groups may be represented. The aim is to secure the services of experts in the appropriate field.

However the board is composed, it is a good idea (and not at all improper or unethical) to ascertain in advance of the interview who the members are and what groups they represent. When you are introduced to them, you will have some idea of their backgrounds and interests, and at least you will not stutter and stammer over their names.

What should be done before the interview?

While knowledge about the board members is useful and takes some of the surprise element out of the interview, there is other preparation which is more substantive. It *is* possible to prepare for an oral interview – in several ways:

1) Keep a copy of your application and review it carefully before the interview

This may be the only document before the oral board, and the starting point of the interview. Know what education and experience you have listed there, and the sequence and dates of all of it. Sometimes the board will ask you to review the highlights of your experience for them; you should not have to hem and haw doing it.

2) Study the class specification and the examination announcement

Usually, the oral board has one or both of these to guide them. The qualities, characteristics or knowledges required by the position sought are stated in these documents. They offer valuable clues as to the nature of the oral interview. For example, if the job involves supervisory responsibilities, the announcement will usually indicate that knowledge of modern supervisory methods and the qualifications of the candidate as a supervisor will be tested. If so, you can expect such questions, frequently in the form of a hypothetical situation which you are expected to solve. NEVER go into an oral without knowledge of the duties and responsibilities of the job you seek.

3) Think through each qualification required

Try to visualize the kind of questions you would ask if you were a board member. How well could you answer them? Try especially to appraise your own knowledge and background in each area, *measured against the job sought*, and identify any areas in which you are weak. Be critical and realistic – do not flatter yourself.

4) Do some general reading in areas in which you feel you may be weak

For example, if the job involves supervision and your past experience has NOT, some general reading in supervisory methods and practices, particularly in the field of human relations, might be useful. Do NOT study agency procedures or detailed manuals. The oral board will be testing your understanding and capacity, not your memory.

5) Get a good night's sleep and watch your general health and mental attitude

You will want a clear head at the interview. Take care of a cold or any other minor ailment, and of course, no hangovers.

What should be done on the day of the interview?

Now comes the day of the interview itself. Give yourself plenty of time to get there. Plan to arrive somewhat ahead of the scheduled time, particularly if your appointment is in the fore part of the day. If a previous candidate fails to appear, the board might be ready for you a bit early. By early afternoon an oral board is almost invariably behind schedule if there are many candidates, and you may have to wait. Take along a book or magazine to read, or your application to review, but leave any extraneous material in the waiting room when you go in for your interview. In any event, relax and compose yourself.

The matter of dress is important. The board is forming impressions about you – from your experience, your manners, your attitude, and your appearance. Give your personal appearance careful attention. Dress your best, but not your flashiest. Choose conservative, appropriate clothing, and be sure it is immaculate. This is a business interview, and your appearance should indicate that you regard it as such. Besides, being well groomed and properly dressed will help boost your confidence.

Sooner or later, someone will call your name and escort you into the interview room. *This is it.* From here on you are on your own. It is too late for any more preparation. But remember, you asked for this opportunity to prove your fitness, and you are here because your request was granted.

What happens when you go in?

The usual sequence of events will be as follows: The clerk (who is often the board stenographer) will introduce you to the chairman of the oral board, who will introduce you to the other members of the board. Acknowledge the introductions before you sit down. Do not be surprised if you find a microphone facing you or a stenotypist sitting by. Oral interviews are usually recorded in the event of an appeal or other review.

Usually the chairman of the board will open the interview by reviewing the highlights of your education and work experience from your application – primarily for the benefit of the other members of the board, as well as to get the material into the record. Do not interrupt or comment unless there is an error or significant misinterpretation; if that is the case, do not hesitate. But do not quibble about insignificant matters. Also, he will usually ask you some question about your education, experience or your present job – partly to get you to start talking and to establish the interviewing "rapport." He may start the actual questioning, or turn it over to one of the other members. Frequently, each member undertakes the questioning on a particular area, one in which he is perhaps most competent, so you can expect each member to participate in the examination. Because time is limited, you may also expect some rather abrupt switches in the direction the questioning takes, so do not be upset by it. Normally, a board member will not pursue a single line of questioning unless he discovers a particular strength or weakness.

After each member has participated, the chairman will usually ask whether any member has any further questions, then will ask you if you have anything you wish to add. Unless you are expecting this question, it may floor you. Worse, it may start you off on an extended, extemporaneous speech. The board is not usually seeking more information. The question is principally to offer you a last opportunity to present further qualifications or to indicate that you have nothing to add. So, if you feel that a significant qualification or characteristic has been overlooked, it is proper to point it out in a sentence or so. Do not compliment the board on the thoroughness of their examination – they have been sketchy, and you know it. If you wish, merely say, "No thank you, I have nothing further to add." This is a point where you can "talk yourself out" of a good impression or fail to present an important bit of information. Remember, *you close the interview yourself*.

The chairman will then say, "That is all, Mr. _____, thank you." Do not be startled; the interview is over, and quicker than you think. Thank him, gather your belongings and take your leave. Save your sigh of relief for the other side of the door.

How to put your best foot forward

Throughout this entire process, you may feel that the board individually and collectively is trying to pierce your defenses, seek out your hidden weaknesses and embarrass and confuse you. Actually, this is not true. They are obliged to make an appraisal of your qualifications for the job you are seeking, and they want to see you in your best light. Remember, they must interview all candidates and a non-cooperative candidate may become a failure in spite of their best efforts to bring out his qualifications. Here are 15 suggestions that will help you:

1) Be natural – Keep your attitude confident, not cocky

If you are not confident that you can do the job, do not expect the board to be. Do not apologize for your weaknesses, try to bring out your strong points. The board is interested in a positive, not negative, presentation. Cockiness will antagonize any board member and make him wonder if you are covering up a weakness by a false show of strength.

2) Get comfortable, but don't lounge or sprawl

Sit erectly but not stiffly. A careless posture may lead the board to conclude that you are careless in other things, or at least that you are not impressed by the importance of the occasion. Either conclusion is natural, even if incorrect. Do not fuss with your clothing, a pencil or an ashtray. Your hands may occasionally be useful to emphasize a point; do not let them become a point of distraction.

3) Do not wisecrack or make small talk

This is a serious situation, and your attitude should show that you consider it as such. Further, the time of the board is limited – they do not want to waste it, and neither should you.

4) Do not exaggerate your experience or abilities

In the first place, from information in the application or other interviews and sources, the board may know more about you than you think. Secondly, you probably will not get away with it. An experienced board is rather adept at spotting such a situation, so do not take the chance.

5) If you know a board member, do not make a point of it, yet do not hide it

Certainly you are not fooling him, and probably not the other members of the board. Do not try to take advantage of your acquaintanceship – it will probably do you little good.

6) Do not dominate the interview

Let the board do that. They will give you the clues – do not assume that you have to do all the talking. Realize that the board has a number of questions to ask you, and do not try to take up all the interview time by showing off your extensive knowledge of the answer to the first one.

7) Be attentive

You only have 20 minutes or so, and you should keep your attention at its sharpest throughout. When a member is addressing a problem or question to you, give him your undivided attention. Address your reply principally to him, but do not exclude the other board members.

8) Do not interrupt

A board member may be stating a problem for you to analyze. He will ask you a question when the time comes. Let him state the problem, and wait for the question.

9) Make sure you understand the question

Do not try to answer until you are sure what the question is. If it is not clear, restate it in your own words or ask the board member to clarify it for you. However, do not haggle about minor elements.

10) Reply promptly but not hastily

A common entry on oral board rating sheets is "candidate responded readily," or "candidate hesitated in replies." Respond as promptly and quickly as you can, but do not jump to a hasty, ill-considered answer.

11) Do not be peremptory in your answers

A brief answer is proper – but do not fire your answer back. That is a losing game from your point of view. The board member can probably ask questions much faster than you can answer them.

12) Do not try to create the answer you think the board member wants

He is interested in what kind of mind you have and how it works – not in playing games. Furthermore, he can usually spot this practice and will actually grade you down on it.

13) Do not switch sides in your reply merely to agree with a board member

Frequently, a member will take a contrary position merely to draw you out and to see if you are willing and able to defend your point of view. Do not start a debate, yet do not surrender a good position. If a position is worth taking, it is worth defending.

14) Do not be afraid to admit an error in judgment if you are shown to be wrong

The board knows that you are forced to reply without any opportunity for careful consideration. Your answer may be demonstrably wrong. If so, admit it and get on with the interview.

15) Do not dwell at length on your present job

The opening question may relate to your present assignment. Answer the question but do not go into an extended discussion. You are being examined for a *new* job, not your present one. As a matter of fact, try to phrase ALL your answers in terms of the job for which you are being examined.

Basis of Rating

Probably you will forget most of these "do's" and "don'ts" when you walk into the oral interview room. Even remembering them all will not ensure you a passing grade. Perhaps you did not have the qualifications in the first place. But remembering them will help you to put your best foot forward, without treading on the toes of the board members.

Rumor and popular opinion to the contrary notwithstanding, an oral board wants you to make the best appearance possible. They know you are under pressure – but they also want to see how you respond to it as a guide to what your reaction would be under the pressures of the job you seek. They will be influenced by the degree of poise you display, the personal traits you show and the manner in which you respond.

ABOUT THIS BOOK

This book contains tests divided into Examination Sections. Go through each test, answering every question in the margin. We have also attached a sample answer sheet at the back of the book that can be removed and used. At the end of each test look at the answer key and check your answers. On the ones you got wrong, look at the right answer choice and learn. Do not fill in the answers first. Do not memorize the questions and answers, but understand the answer and principles involved. On your test, the questions will likely be different from the samples. Questions are changed and new ones added. If you understand these past questions you should have success with any changes that arise. Tests may consist of several types of questions. We have additional books on each subject should more study be advisable or necessary for you. Finally, the more you study, the better prepared you will be. This book is intended to be the last thing you study before you walk into the examination room. Prior study of relevant texts is also recommended. NLC publishes some of these in our Fundamental Series. Knowledge and good sense are important factors in passing your exam. Good luck also helps. So now study this Passbook, absorb the material contained within and take that knowledge into the examination. Then do your best to pass that exam.

EXAMINATION SECTION

EXAMINATION SECTION
TEST 1

DIRECTIONS: Each question or incomplete statement is followed by several suggested answers or completions. Select the one that BEST answers the question or completes the statement. *PRINT THE LETTER OF THE CORRECT ANSWER IN THE SPACE AT THE RIGHT.*

Questions 1-8.

DIRECTIONS: Questions 1 through 8 involve tests on the fuse box arrangement shown below. All tests are to be performed with a neon tester or a lamp test bank consisting of two 6-watt, 120-volt lamps connected in series. Do not make any assumptions about the conditions of the circuits. Draw your conclusions only from the information obtained with the neon tester or the two-lamp test bank, applied to the circuits as called for.

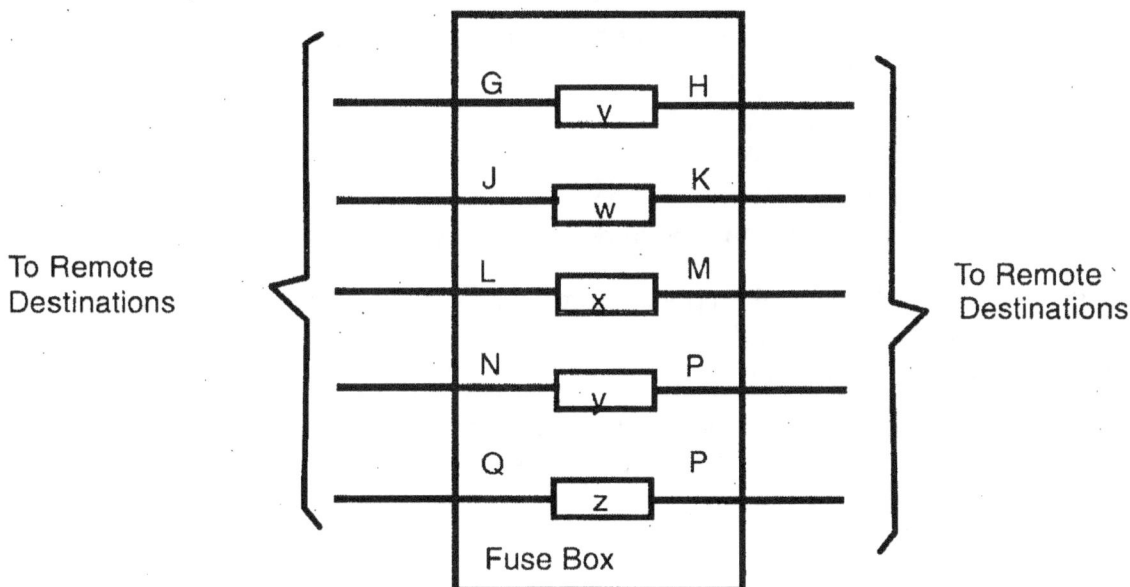

1. The two lamp test bank is placed from point G to joint J, and both lamps light. One of the lamps is momentarily removed from its socket; during that instant, the other lamp in the series-connected test bank should

    A. go dark   B. get dimmer
    C. remain at same brightness   D. get brighter

1.____

2. The test bank with two 60-watt, 120-volt lamps in series should be used on circuits with

    A. wattages only from 60 to 120 watts
    B. wattages only from 0 to 120 watts
    C. voltages only from 120 to 240 volts
    D. voltages only from 0 to 240 volts

2.____

3. The neon tester is placed from point G to point J and only one-half of the neon tester lights.
It should be concluded that

   A. half of the tester has gone bad
   B. a wire has become disconnected in the circuit
   C. the voltage is AC
   D. the voltage is DC

3.____

4. If both lamps in the test bank light when placed directly across one of the above fuses, it should be concluded that

   A. the fuse is good
   B. the fuse is blown
   C. the fuse is overrated
   D. further tests have to be made to determine the condition of the fuse

4.____

5. If the lamp test bank does not light when placed directly across one of the above fuses, it should be concluded that

   A. the fuse is good
   B. the fuse is blown
   C. the fuse is overrated
   D. further tests have to be made to determine the condition of the fuse

5.____

6. The lamp test bank lights when placed from point G to point J but does not light when placed from point H to point J.
It should be concluded that

   A. the wire to point H has become disconnected
   B. the wire to point J has become disconnected
   C. fuse v is bad
   D. fuse w is bad

6.____

7. The lamp test bank lights when placed from point L to point N but does not light when placed from point M to point P.
It should be concluded that

   A. both fuses x and y are bad
   B. either fuse x or fuse y is bad or both are bad
   C. both fuses x and y are good
   D. these tests do not indicate the condition of any fuse

7.____

8. The lamp test bank is placed from point L to point N, then from N to point Q, and finally from point L to point Q. In each case, both lamps light to full brightness.
It should be concluded that points L, N, and Q have

   A. three-phase, 120 volts, AC, line-to-line
   B. plus and minus 120 volts, DC
   C. three-phase, 208 volts, AC
   D. plus and minus 240 volts, DC

8.____

9. An automatic device used for regulating air temperature is a(n)

   A. rheostat   B. aquastat   C. thermostat   D. duostat

10. Assume that you have just completed a certain maintenance job which you feel is satisfactory, but your foreman asks you to make certain changes.
    The BEST procedure for you to follow is to

    A. request the foreman to assign this work to someone else
    B. have another maintainer verify that the job was done properly
    C. ask the foreman the reasons for the changes
    D. complain to the foreman's superior of this waste of time

11. The PROPER set of tools and equipment to be used to clean and adjust the ignition points of an automobile consists of a

    A. screwdriver, feeler gauge, and point file
    B. wrench, micrometer, and sandpaper
    C. scraper, micrometer, and emery cloth
    D. V-block, pliers, and sandpaper

12. The voltage developed in each cell of an automobile battery is _____ volts.

    A. 2   B. 4   C. 6   D. 12

13. The one of the following tools that is NOT used to clear plumbing stoppages is a

    A. force-cup   B. drain auger
    C. snake   D. pick-out iron

14. Eyebolts are generally fastened to the shells of machinery in order to

    A. act as a leveling device
    B. facilitate lifting
    C. permit easy tagging of the equipment
    D. reinforce the machine shells

15. When grinding a weld smooth, it is MOST important to avoid

    A. grinding too slowly
    B. overheating the surrounding metal
    C. grinding away too much of the weld
    D. grinding after the weld has cooled off

16. A cold chisel whose head has become *mushroomed* should NOT be used because

    A. it is impossible to hit the head squarely
    B. the chisel will not cut accurately
    C. chips might fly from the head
    D. the chisel has lost its *temper*

17. The type of screwdriver specially made to be used in tight spots is the

    A. Phillips   B. offset
    C. square shank   D. truss

18. An indication that a fluorescent lamp in a fixture should be replaced is 18.____
    A. humming in the fixture
    B. the ends of the lamp remain black when the lamp is lit
    C. poor or slow starting
    D. the lamp does not shut off each time the OFF button is pressed

19. Asbestos is used as a covering on electrical wires to provide protection from 19.____
    A. high voltage   B. high temperatures
    C. water damage   D. electrolysis

20. Many electric power tools, such as drills, have a third conductor in the line cord which 20.____
    should be connected to a grounded part of the power receptacle.
    The reason for this is to
    A. have a spare wire in case one power wire should break
    B. strengthen the power lead so that it cannot be easily damaged
    C. protect the user of the tool from electrical shocks
    D. allow use of the tool for extended periods of time without overheating

21. Employees are responsible for the good care, proper maintenance, and serviceable con- 21.____
    dition of the property issued or assigned for their use.
    As used above, *serviceable condition* means the property is in a state where it is
    A. capable of being repaired   B. easily handled
    C. fit for use   D. least expensive

22. A brush that has been used in shellac should be cleaned by washing it in 22.____
    A. water   B. linseed oil
    C. lacquer thinner   D. alcohol

23. Excessive moisture on a surface being painted would MOST likely result in 23.____
    A. alligatoring   B. blistering
    C. cracking   D. sagging

24. In order to reverse the direction of rotation of a series motor, the 24.____
    A. connections to the armature should be reversed
    B. connections to both the armature and the series field should be reversed
    C. connections of the motor to the power lines should be reversed
    D. series field should be placed in shunt with the armature

25. A megger is an instrument used to measure 25.____
    A. capacitance   B. insulation resistance
    C. power   D. illumination levels

26. The first aid treatment for chemical burns on the skin is 26.____
    A. treatment with ointment and then bandaging
    B. washing with large quantities of water and then treating as heat burns
    C. treatment with a neutralizing agent and no bandaging
    D. application of sodium bicarbonate and then bandaging

27. The chemical MOST frequently used to clean drains clogged with grease is   27.____

    A. muriatic acid   B. soda ash
    C. ammonia   D. caustic soda

28. When tapping a blind hole in a steel plate, the FIRST type of tap to use is a _____ tap.   28.____

    A. plug   B. taper   C. lead   D. bottoming

29. A common handshaving tool used in woodwork is a(n)   29.____

    A. trammel   B. router   C. auger   D. plane

30. *Dressing* a grinding wheel refers to   30.____

    A. making the wheel thinner
    B. replacing with a new wheel
    C. repairing a crack in the wheel
    D. making the wheel round

31. The maintainer who is MOST valuable is the one who   31.____

    A. offers to do the heavy lifting
    B. asks many questions about the work
    C. listens to instructions and carries them out
    D. makes many suggestions on work procedures

32. Of the following, turpentine is used for thinning   32.____

    A. latex paint   B. red lead paint
    C. calcimine   D. shellac

33. Of the following, the hacksaw blade BEST suited for cutting thin-walled tubing is one   33.____
    which has _____ teeth/inch.

    A. 14   B. 18   C. 24   D. 32

34. Because of its weather-resistant properties, a varnish commonly used on exterior sur-   34.____
    faces is _____ varnish.

    A. spar   B. flat   C. rubbing   D. hard oil

35. A trip spring or spring cylinder on a snow plow assembly is a device that   35.____

    A. absorbs the shock of impact when the plow strikes an obstacle in the road
    B. provides for snap-action in the lowering of the plow blade
    C. allows for quick removal or attachment of the snow plow supporting frame
    D. detaches the plow blade and lets it hang free when the plow blade is dragged
       backwards

36. The term *preventative maintenance* is used to identify a plan whereby   36.____

    A. equipment is serviced according to a regular schedule
    B. equipment is serviced as soon as it fails
    C. equipment is replaced as soon as it becomes obsolete
    D. all equipment is replaced periodically

37. The ratio of air to gasoline in an automobile engine is controlled by the

     A. gas filter	B. fuel pump
     C. carburetor	D. intake manifold

38. *Energizer* is another name given to the

     A. automobile battery	B. fluorescent fixture ballast
     C. battery charger	D. generator shunt field

39. Wearshoes may be found on

     A. circuit breakers	B. automobile brake systems
     C. snow plows	D. door sills

40. When moving heavy equipment by means of pipe rollers, it is MOST important to

     A. use solid steel rollers
     B. use rollers with different diameters
     C. see that the trailing roller does not slip out from under the equipment
     D. use more than three rollers at all times

41. The one of the following storage areas that is BEST for the storage of paint is one which is

     A. unheated and not ventilated
     B. cool and ventilated
     C. sunny and ventilated
     D. warm and not ventilated

42. The leverage that can be obtained with a wrench is determined mainly by the

     A. material of which the wrench is made
     B. gripping surface of the jaw
     C. length of the handle
     D. thickness of the wrench

43. A star drill is used to bore holes in

     A. steel	B. concrete	C. wood	D. sheet metal

44. The one of the following actions of a maintainer that is MOST likely to contribute to a good working relationship between him and his assistant is for him to

     A. observe the same rules of conduct that he expects his assistant to observe
     B. freely give advice on his assistant's personal problems
     C. always be frank and outspoken to his assistant in pointing out his faults
     D. expect his assistant to perform with equal efficiency on any job assigned

45. Three common types of windows are

     A. batten, casement, and awning
     B. batten, casement, and double-hung
     C. batten, double-hung, and awning
     D. casement, double-hung, and awning

46. A staircase has twelve risers, each 6 3/4" high. The TOTAL rise of the staircase is

   A. 6'2 1/4"   B. 6'9"   C. 7'0"   D. 7'3 3/4"

47. A twenty-foot straight ladder placed at an angle against a wall should be at a distance from the wall equal to _____ feet.

   A. 3   B. 5   C. 7   D. 9

48. Reflective sheeting traffic signs that have become dirty should be wiped with kerosene or gasoline FOLLOWED by a

   A. wiping with a soft cloth soaked in thin oil
   B. hand rub with very fine sandpaper
   C. wash with detergent and a rinse with water
   D. coating of shellac applied with a brush

49. A temporary wooden fence carrying red flags and built around an opening in a pavement to warn oncoming traffic is known as a

   A. batter board   B. bulkhead
   C. bollard   D. barricade

50. *Four-ply belted* is used to describe the construction of

   A. belt-drive pulleys
   B. auto tires
   C. electrical wiring insulation
   D. seat belts

KEY (CORRECT ANSWERS)

1. A	11. A	21. C	31. C	41. B
2. D	12. A	22. D	32. B	42. C
3. D	13. D	23. B	33. D	43. B
4. B	14. B	24. A	34. A	44. A
5. D	15. C	25. B	35. A	45. D
6. C	16. C	26. B	36. A	46. B
7. B	17. B	27. D	37. C	47. B
8. C	18. B	28. B	38. A	48. C
9. C	19. B	29. D	39. C	49. D
10. C	20. C	30. D	40. C	50. B

TEST 2

DIRECTIONS: Each question or incomplete statement is followed by several suggested answers or completions. Select the one that BEST answers the question or completes the statement. *PRINT THE LETTER OF THE CORRECT ANSWER IN THE SPACE AT THE RIGHT.*

1. An oil bath filter is MOST often used on a(n)
    A. air compressor
    B. auto engine
    C. electric generator
    D. steam boiler

2. A 3-ohm resistor placed across a 12-volt battery will dissipate _____ watts.
    A. 3   B. 4   C. 12   D. 48

3. Instead of using fuses, modern electric wiring uses
    A. quick switches
    B. circuit breakers
    C. fusible links
    D. lag blocks

4. The MOST common combination of gases used for welding is
    A. carbon dioxide and acetylene
    B. nitrogen and hydrogen
    C. oxygen and acetylene
    D. oxygen and hydrogen

5. If a wheel has turned through an angle of 180, then it has made _____ revolution(s).
    A. 1/4   B. 1/2   C. 1/8   D. 18

6. Sewer gas is prevented from backing up through a plumbing fixture by a
    A. water trap
    B. return elbow
    C. check valve
    D. float valve

7. Putty that is too stiff is made workable by adding
    A. gasoline
    B. linseed oil
    C. water
    D. lacquer thinner

8. A vertical wood member in the wall of a wood frame house is known as a
    A. A stringer
    B. ridge member
    C. stud
    D. header

9. A 10-to-1 step-down transformer has an input of 1 ampere at 120 volts AC. If the losses are negligible, the output of the transformer is _____ volts.
    A. 1 ampere at 12
    B. .1 ampere at 1200
    C. 10 amperes at 12
    D. 10 amperes at 120

10. An oscilloscope is an instrument used in
    A. measuring noise levels
    B. displaying waveforms of electrical signals
    C. indicating the concentrations of pollutants in air
    D. photographing high-speed events

11. Assume that a brake pedal of a truck goes to the floorboard when depressed. The one of the following that could cause this condition is

    A. a leak in the hydraulic lines
    B. a clogged hydraulic line
    C. scored drums
    D. glazed linings

12. The universal joints of an automobile are located on the

    A. suspension springs   B. steering linkages
    C. wheel cylinders   D. drive shaft

13. The MAIN purpose of a flexible coupling is to connect two shafts which are

    A. of different diameters   B. of different shapes
    C. not in exact alignment   D. of different material

14. When using a standard measuring micrometer, starting with a zero reading, one complete counterclockwise revolution of the sleeve will give a reading of _____ inch.

    A. .001   B. .010   C. .025   D. .250

15. If a nut is to be tightened to an exact specified value of inch-lbs., the wrench to use is a _____ wrench.

    A. spanner   B. box   C. lock-jaw D. torque

16. Common permanent type anti-freezes for automobile cooling systems are MAINLY

    A. alcohol   B. methanol
    C. ethylene glycol   D. trychloroethylene

17. Plexiglas is also called

    A. mylar   B. lucite   C. isinglass D. PVC

18. Long, curved lines are BEST cut in 1/4" plexiglas with a _____ saw.

    A. rip   B. jig   C. keyhole   D. coping

19. The specific gravity of storage battery cells can be measured with a(n)

    A. odometer B. hydrometer C. ammeter D. dwell meter

20. A nail set is a tool used for

    A. straightening bent nails
    B. measuring nail sizes
    C. cutting nails to specified size
    D. driving a nail head into wood

21. To cut a number of 2" x 4" lengths of wood accurately at an angle of 45°, it is BEST to use a

    A. protractor B. mitre-box C. triangle D. square

22. The type of fastener MOST commonly used when bolting to concrete uses a(n)

    A. expansion shield B. U-bolt
    C. toggle bolt D. turnbuckle

23. When an automobile engine does not start on a damp day, the trouble is MOST likely in the _____ system.

    A. ignition B. cooling C. fuel D. lubricating

24. The battery of an automobile is prevented from discharging back through the alternator by the blocking action of the

    A. commutator B. diodes C. brushes D. slip rings

25. The master cylinder in an automobile is actuated by the

    A. steering column B. brake pedal
    C. clutch plate D. cam shaft

26. The FINEST sandpaper from among the following is No.

    A. 3 B. 1 C. 2/0 D. 6/0

27. A screw whose head is buried below the surface of the wood that it is screwed into is said to be

    A. countersunk B. scalloped
    C. expanded D. flushed

28. The one of the following devices which is used to measure angles is the

    A. caliper B. protractor
    C. marking gauge D. divider

29. Before a new oil stone is used, it should be

    A. heated B. soaked in oil
    C. coated with shellac D. washed with soapy water

30. Dies are used for

    A. threading the outside ends of metal pipes
    B. making sweated joints on lead pipes
    C. cutting nipples to exact lengths
    D. caulking cast-iron pipe joints

31. The energy stored by a storage battery is commonly given in

    A. volts B. amperes
    C. ampere-hours D. kilowatts

32. *Vapor lock* occurs in automobile

    A. gas tanks B. crankcases
    C. transmissions D. carburetors

33. A woodworking tool used to bore odd-size holes for which there is no standard auger bit is a(n)

    A. single twist auger   B. double twist auger
    C. expansive bit   D. straight fluted drill

34. Soap is sometimes applied to wood screws in order to

    A. prevent rust   B. make a tight fit
    C. make insertion easier   D. prevent wood splitting

35. On a long run of copper tubing, the tubing is often bent in the shape of a horseshoe rather than being run in a straight line.
The MAIN reason for this is to

    A. allow an excess that could be used in future repairs
    B. make it easier to install the tubing
    C. permit the tubing to expand and contract with changes in temperature
    D. eliminate the need for accurate measurements in cutting the tubing

36. Loss of seal water in a house water trap is prevented by the use of a

    A. drainage tee   B. faucet   C. hose bibb   D. vent

37. BX is a designation for a type of

    A. flexible armored electric cable
    B. flexible gas line
    C. rigid conduit
    D. electrical insulation

38. *WYE-WYE* and *DELTA-WYE* are two

    A. types of DC motor windings
    B. arrangements of 3-phase transformer connections
    C. types of electrical splices
    D. shapes of commutator bars

39. Green lumber should NOT be used in the building of scaffolding because it

    A. will not hold nails well
    B. easily splits when nailed
    C. may warp on drying
    D. is too expensive

40. *Scotchlite* ready-made traffic sign faces with heat-activated adhesive backings are applied to backing blanks by use of a

    A. temperature-controlled oven
    B. vacuum applicator
    C. hot water bath
    D. heated roller assembly

41. *Scotchcal* is a(n)

    A. reflective sheeting   B. epoxy protective paint
    C. fluorescent film   D. high temperature lubricant

42. Wooden ladders should NOT be painted because the paint   42.___

    A. is inflammable
    B. may cover defects in the wood
    C. makes the rungs slippery
    D. may deteriorate the wood

43. To prevent ladders from slipping, the bottoms of the ladder side rails are OFTEN fitted with   43.___

    A. automatic locks   B. ladder shoes
    C. ladder hooks   D. stirrups

44. A bowline is   44.___

    A. the sag that a scaffold develops when men get on it
    B. a knot with a loop that does not run
    C. a temporary telephone wire strung during emergencies
    D. the reference line established in ditch excavations

45. A method sometimes used to prevent a pipe from buckling during a bending operation is to   45.___

    A. bend the pipe very quickly
    B. keep the seam of the pipe on the outside of the bend
    C. nick the pipe at the center of the bend
    D. pack the inside of the pipe with sand

46. A rectifier changes   46.___

    A. DC to AC
    B. AC to DC
    C. single-phase power to three-phase power
    D. battery power to three-phase power

47. Continuity in a de-energized electrical circuit may be checked with a(n)   47.___

    A. voltmeter   B. ohmmeter   C. neon tester   D. rheostat

48. Of the following crankcase oils, the one that should be used in sub-zero weather is SAE   48.___

    A. 10W   B. 20W   C. 20   D. 30

49. Caster in an automobile is an adjustment in the   49.___

    A. ignition system   B. drive-shaft
    C. rear differential   D. front suspension

50. If the spark plugs in an engine run too hot, the result is MOST likely that   50.___

    A. oil and carbon compounds will accumulate on the insulators
    B. the electrodes will wear rapidly
    C. the timing will be retarded
    D. the ignition coil may become damaged

KEY (CORRECT ANSWERS)

1. B	11. A	21. B	31. C	41. C
2. B	12. D	22. A	32. D	42. B
3. B	13. C	23. A	33. C	43. B
4. C	14. C	24. B	34. C	44. B
5. B	15. D	25. B	35. C	45. D
6. A	16. C	26. D	36. D	46. B
7. B	17. B	27. A	37. A	47. B
8. C	18. B	28. B	38. B	48. A
9. C	19. B	29. B	39. C	49. D
10. B	20. D	30. A	40. B	50. B

EXAMINATION SECTION
TEST 1

DIRECTIONS: Each question or incomplete statement is followed by several suggested answers or completions. Select the one that BEST answers the question or completes the statement. *PRINT THE LETTER OF THE CORRECT ANSWER IN THE SPACE AT THE RIGHT.*

1. A bit is held in a hand drill by means of a(n)

    A. arbor B. chuck C. collet D. clamp

2. The type of screw that MOST often requires a countersunk hole is a _____ head.

    A. flat B. round C. fillister D. hexagon

3. Instead of using the ordinary 1 piece screwdriver, a screwdriver bit is MOST often used with a brace because of the

    A. increased length of the brace
    B. different types of bits available
    C. increased leverage of the brace
    D. ability to work in tight corners

4. A thread gage is usually used to measure the

    A. thickness of a thread
    B. diameter of a thread
    C. number of threads per inch
    D. height of a thread

5. The wheel of a glass cutter is BEST lubricated with

    A. kerosene
    B. linseed oil
    C. varnolene
    D. diesel oil

6. A nail set is a

    A. group of nails of the same size and type
    B. group of nails of different sizes but the same type
    C. tool used to extract nails
    D. tool used to drive nails below the surface of wood

7. To test for leaks in a gas line, it is BEST to use

    A. a match
    B. soapy water
    C. a colored dye
    D. ammonia

8. Routing is the process of cutting a

    A. strip out of sheet metal
    B. groove in wood
    C. chamfer on a shaft
    D. core out of concrete

9. A hacksaw frame has a wing nut mainly to

    A. make it easier to replace blades
    B. increase the strength of the frame
    C. prevent vibration of the blade
    D. adjust the length of the frame

10. A mitre box is usually used with a _____ saw.

    A. hack   B. crosscut   C. rip   D. back

11. A continuous flexible saw blade is MOST often used on a _____ saw.

    A. radial   B. band   C. swing   D. table

12. A pipe reamer is used to

    A. clean out a length of pipe
    B. thread pipe
    C. remove burrs from the ends of pipe
    D. seal pipe joints

13. To lay out a straight cut on a piece of wood at the same angle as the cut on a second piece of wood, the PROPER tool to use is a

    A. bevel   B. cope   C. butt gauge   D. clevis

14. Before drilling a hole in a piece of metal, an indentation should be made with a _____ punch.

    A. pin   B. taper   C. center   D. drift

15. Curved cuts in wood are BEST made with a _____ saw.

    A. jig   B. veneer   C. radial   D. swing

16. A face plate is generally used to

    A. hold material while working with it on a lathe
    B. smooth out irregularities in a metal plate
    C. protect the finish on a metal plate
    D. locate centers of holes to be drilled on a drill press

17. A die would be used to

    A. gage the groove in a splined shaft
    B. cut a thread on a metal rod
    C. hold a piece to be machined on a milling machine
    D. control the depth of a hole to be drilled in a piece of metal

18. Before using a ladle to scoop up molten solder, you should make sure that the ladle is dry.
    This is done to prevent

    A. the solder from sticking to the ladle
    B. impurities from getting into the solder
    C. injuries due to splashing solder
    D. cooling of the solder

19. To PROPERLY adjust the gap on a spark plug, you should use a(n)   19.____
    A. inside caliper   B. center gauge
    C. wire type feeler gauge   D. micrometer

20. The length of the MOST common type of folding wood rule is _____ feet.   20.____
    A. 4   B. 5   C. 6   D. 7

21. A four-foot mason's level is usually used to determine whether the top of a wall is level and whether it is   21.____
    A. square   B. plumb   C. rigid   D. in line

22. To match a tongue in a board, the matching board MUST have a   22.____
    A. rabbet   B. chamfer   C. bead   D. groove

23. When driving screws in close quarters, the BEST type of screwdriver to use is a(n)   23.____
    A. Phillips   B. offset   C. butt   D. angled

24. The term 12-24 refers to a _____ screw.   24.____
    A. wood   B. lag
    C. sheet metal   D. machine

25. To measure the length of a curved line on a drawing or plan, the PROPER tool to use in addition to a ruler is(are)   25.____
    A. dividers   B. calipers
    C. surface gage   D. radius gage

26. For the standard machine screw, the diameter of a tap drill is generally   26.____
    A. *equal* to the diameter of the shaft of the screw at the base of the threads (the root diameter)
    B. *larger* than the root diameter, but smaller than the diameter of the screw
    C. *equal* to the diameter of the screw
    D. *larger* than the diameter of the screw

27. In order to drill a 1" hole accurately with a drill press, you should   27.____
    A. drill at high speeds
    B. use very little pressure on the drill
    C. drill partway down, release pressure on the drill, and then continue drilling
    D. drill a pilot hole first

28. Before taking apart an electric motor to repair, punch marks are sometimes placed on the casing near each other.   28.____
    The MOST probable reason for doing this is to
    A. make sure the parts lock together on reassembly
    B. properly line up the parts that are next to each other
    C. keep track of the number of parts in the assembly
    D. identify all the parts as coming from the one motor

29. To locate a point on a floor directly under a point on the ceiling, the PROPER tool to use is a 29.____

   A. square
   B. line level
   C. height gage
   D. plumb bob

Question 30.

DIRECTIONS: Question 30 is based on the diagram appearing below.

30. In the above diagram, the full P required to lift the weight a distance of four feet is MOST NEARLY _____ lbs. 30.____

   A. 50 B. 67 C. 75 D. 100

31. The EASIEST tool to use to determine whether the edge of a board is at right angles to the face of the board is a 31.____

   A. rafter square
   B. try square
   C. protractor
   D. marking gage

32. *Whetting* refers to 32.____

   A. tempering of tools by dipping them in water
   B. annealing of tools by heating and slow cooling
   C. brazing of carbide tips on tools
   D. sharpening of tools

33. The MOST difficult part of a plank to plane is the 33.____

   A. face B. side C. end D. back

34. To prevent wood from splitting when drilling with an auger, it is BEST to 34.____

   A. use even pressure on the bit
   B. drill at a slow speed
   C. hold the wood tightly in a vise
   D. back up the wood with a piece of scrap wood

35. The term *dressing a grinding wheel* refers to 35.____

    A. setting up the wheel on the arbor
    B. restoring the sharpness of a wheel face that has become clogged
    C. placing flanges against the sides of the wheel
    D. bringing the wheel up to speed before using it

36. Heads of rivets are BEST cut off with a 36.____

    A. hacksaw   B. cold chisel
    C. fly cutter   D. reamer

37. A *V-block* is especially useful to 37.____

    A. prevent damage to work held in a vise
    B. hold round stock while a hole is being drilled into it
    C. prevent rolling of round stock stored on the ground
    D. shim up the end of a machine so that it is level

38. A full set of taps for a given size usually consists of a _____ tap. 38.____

    A. taper and bottoming
    B. taper and plug
    C. plug and bottoming
    D. taper, plug, and bottoming

39. Round thread cutting dies are usually held in stock by means of 39.____

    A. wing nuts   B. clamps   C. set screws   D. bolts

40. The one of the following diagrams that shows the plan view and the elevation of a counterbored hole is 40.____

A.

B.

C.

D.

41. With regard to pipe, *I.D.* usually means 41.____

    A. inside diameter   B. inside dressed
    C. invert diameter   D. installation date

42. A compression fitting is MOST often used to

    A. lubricate a wheel
    B. join two pieces of tubing
    C. reduce the diameter of a hole
    D. press fit a gear to a shaft

43. The shape of a mill file is basically

    A. flat   B. half round   C. triangular   D. square

44. Of the following, the ratio of tin to lead that will produce the solder with the LOWEST melting point is

    A. 30-70   B. 40-60   C. 50-50   D. 60-40

45. A safe edge on a file is one that

    A. is smooth and can not cut
    B. has a finer cut than the face of the file
    C. is rounded to prevent scratches
    D. has a coarser cut than the face of the file

46. The MOST frequent use of a file card is to _____ files.

    A. sort out
    B. clean
    C. prevent damage to
    D. prevent clogging of

47. The BEST way of determining whether a grinding wheel has an internal crack is to

    A. run the wheel at high speed, stop it, and examine the wheel
    B. spray lubricating oil on the sides of the wheel and check the amount of absorption of the oil
    C. hit the wheel with a rubber hammer and listen to the sound
    D. drop the wheel sharply on a table and then check the wheel

48. If a grinding wheel has worn to a smaller diameter, the BEST practice to follow is to

    A. discard the wheel
    B. continue using the wheel as before
    C. use the wheel, but at a faster speed
    D. use the wheel, but at a slower speed

49. With respect to the ordinary awl,

    A. only the tip is hardened
    B. the entire blade is hardened
    C. the tip is tempered, and the rest of the blade is hardened
    D. the entire blade is tempered

50. To prevent overheating of drills, it is BEST to use _____ oil.

    A. cutting
    B. lubricating
    C. penetrating
    D. heating

KEY (CORRECT ANSWERS)

1. B	11. B	21. B	31. B	41. A
2. A	12. C	22. D	32. D	42. B
3. C	13. A	23. B	33. C	43. A
4. C	14. C	24. D	34. D	44. D
5. A	15. A	25. A	35. B	45. A
6. D	16. A	26. B	36. B	46. B
7. B	17. B	27. D	37. B	47. C
8. B	18. C	28. B	38. D	48. C
9. A	19. C	29. D	39. C	49. A
10. D	20. C	30. D	40. A	50. A

TEST 2

DIRECTIONS: Each question or incomplete statement is followed by several suggested answers or completions. Select the one that BEST answers the question or completes the statement. *PRINT THE LETTER OF THE CORRECT ANSWER IN THE SPACE AT THE RIGHT.*

1. Crocus cloth is commonly used to   1.____
   - A. protect finely machined surfaces from damage while the machines are being repaired
   - B. remove rust from steel
   - C. protect floors and furniture while painting walls
   - D. wipe up oil and grease that has spilled

2. Before using a new paint brush, the FIRST operation should be to   2.____
   - A. remove loose bristles
   - B. soak the brush in linseed oil
   - C. hang the brush up overnight
   - D. clean the brush with turpentine

3. When sharpening a hand saw, the FIRST operation is to   3.____
   - A. file the teeth down to the same height
   - B. shape the teeth to the proper profile
   - C. bend the teeth over to provide clearance when sawing
   - D. clean the gullies with a file

4. To prevent solder from dripping when soldering a vertical seam, it is BEST to   4.____
   - A. hold a waxed rag under the soldering iron
   - B. use the soldering iron in a horizontal position
   - C. tin the soldering iron on one side only
   - D. solder the seam in the order from bottom to top

5. If a round nut has two holes in the face, the PROPER type wrench to use to tighten this nut is a(n)   5.____
   - A. Stillson   B. monkey   C. spanner   D. open end

6. A box wrench is BEST used on   6.____
   - A. pipe fittings   B. flare nuts
   - C. hexagonal nuts   D. Allen screws

7. To prevent damage to fine finishes on metal work that is to be held in a vise, you should   7.____
   - A. clamp the work lightly
   - B. use brass inserts on the vise
   - C. wrap the work with cloth before inserting it in the vise
   - D. substitute a smooth face plate for the serrated plate on the vise

8. The MOST frequent use for a turnbuckle is to 8._____

    A. tighten a guy wire
    B. adjust shims on a machine
    C. bolt a bracket to a wall
    D. support electric cable from a ceiling

9. To form the head of a tinner's rivet, the PROPER tool to use is a rivet 9._____

    A. anvil   B. plate   C. set   D. brake

10. A socket speed handle MOST closely resembles a 10._____

    A. screwdriver   B. brace   C. spanner   D. spin grip

11. Tips of masonry drills are usually made of 11._____

    A. steel   B. carbide   C. corundum   D. monel

12. The BEST flux to use for soldering galvanized iron is 12._____

    A. resin   B. sal ammoniac
    C. borax   D. muriatic acid

13. The one of the following that is NOT a common type of oilstone is 13._____

    A. silicon carbide   B. aluminum oxide
    C. hard Arkansas   D. pumice

14. A method of joining metals using temperatures intermediate between soldering and welding is 14._____

    A. corbelling   B. brazing   C. annealing   D. lapping

15. When an unusually high degree of accuracy is required with woodwork, lines should be marked with a 15._____

    A. pencil ground to a chisel point
    B. pencil line over a crayon line
    C. sharp knife point
    D. scriber

16. The MOST important difference between pipe threads and V threads on bolts is that pipe threads are usually 16._____

    A. longer   B. sharper
    C. tapered   D. more evenly spaced

17. A street elbow differs from the ordinary elbow in that the street elbow has 17._____

    A. different diameter threads at each end
    B. male threads at one end and female threads at the other
    C. female threads at both ends
    D. male threads at both ends

18. Water hammer in a pipe line can MOST often be stopped by the installation of a(n) 18._____

    A. pressure reducing valve   B. expansion joint
    C. flexible coupling   D. air chamber

19. If water is leaking from the top part of a bibcock, the part that should be replaced is MOST likely the

   A. bibb washer
   B. packing
   C. seat
   D. bibb screw

20. When joining electric wires together in a fixture box, the BEST thing to use are wire

   A. connectors   B. couplings   C. clamps   D. bolts

21. If the name plate of a motor indicates that it is a split phase motor, it is LIKELY that this motor

   A. is a universal motor
   B. operates on DC only
   C. operates on AC only
   D. operates either on DC at full power or on AC at reduced power

22. To make driving of a screw into hard wood easier, it is BEST to lubricate the threads of the screw with

   A. varnoline
   B. penetrating oil
   C. beeswax
   D. cutting oil

23. Assume that a thermostatically controlled oil heater fails to operate. To determine whether it is the thermostat that is at fault, you should

   A. check the circuit breaker
   B. connect a wire across the terminals of the thermostat
   C. replace the contacts on the thermostat
   D. put an ammeter on the line

24. The function of the carburetor on a gasoline engine is to

   A. mix the air and gasoline properly
   B. filter the fuel
   C. filter the air to engine
   D. pump the gasoline into the cylinder

25. If a car owner complains that the battery in his car is constantly running dry, the item that should be checked FIRST is the

   A. fan belt
   B. generator
   C. voltage regulator
   D. relay

26. On MOST modern automobiles, foot brake pressure is transmitted to the brake drums by

   A. air pressure
   B. mechanical linkage
   C. hydraulic fluid
   D. electro-magnetic force

27. Assume that the engine of a car remains cold even though it is run for a period of time. The part that is MOST likely at fault is the

   A. heat by-pass valve
   B. thermostat
   C. heater control
   D. choke

28. To permit easy stripping of concrete forms, they should be 28.____
    A. dried B. oiled C. wet down D. cleaned

29. To prevent honey combing in concrete, the concrete should be 29.____
    A. vibrated
    B. cured
    C. heated in cold weather
    D. protected from the rain

30. The MAIN reason for using wire mesh in connection with concrete work is to 30.____
    A. strain the impurities from the sand
    B. increase the strength of the concrete
    C. hold the forms together
    D. protect the concrete till it hardens

31. Segregation of concrete is MOST often caused by pouring concrete 31.____
    A. in cold weather
    B. from too great a height
    C. too rapidly
    D. into a form in which the concrete has already begun to harden

32. Headers in carpentry are MOST closely associated with 32.____
    A. trimmers B. cantilevers
    C. posts D. newels

33. Joists are very often supported by 33.____
    A. suspenders B. base plates
    C. anchor bolts D. bridal irons

34. At outside corners, the type of joint MOST frequently used on a baseboard is the 34.____
    A. plowed B. mitered
    C. mortise and tenon D. butt

35. The vehicle used with latex paints is usually 35.____
    A. linseed oil B. shellac
    C. varnish D. water

36. *Boxing* of paint refers to the _____ of paints. 36.____
    A. mixing B. storage C. use D. canning

37. When painting wood, nail holes should be puttied 37.____
    A. *before* applying the prime coat
    B. *after* applying the prime coat but before the second coat
    C. *after* applying the second coat but before the third coat
    D. *after* applying the third coat

38. In laying up a brick wall, you find that at the end of the wall there is not enough space for a full brick. 38.____
    You should use a

    A. stretcher B. bat C. corbel D. bull nose

39. Pointing a brick wall is the same as

   A. truing up the wall
   B. topping the wall with a waterproof surface
   C. repairing the mortar joints in the wall
   D. providing a foundation for the wall

39.____

40. The pigment MOST often used in a prime coat of paint on steel to prevent rusting is

   A. lampblack
   B. calcimine
   C. zinc oxide
   D. red lead

40.____

41. If you find a co-worker lying unconscious across an electric wire, the FIRST thing you should do is

   A. get him off the wire
   B. call the foreman
   C. get a doctor
   D. shut off the power

41.____

42.

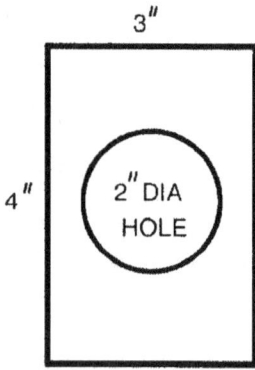

The area of the metal plate shown above, minus the hole area, is MOST NEARLY _____ square inches.

A. 8.5   B. 8.9   C. 9.4   D. 10.1

42.____

43.

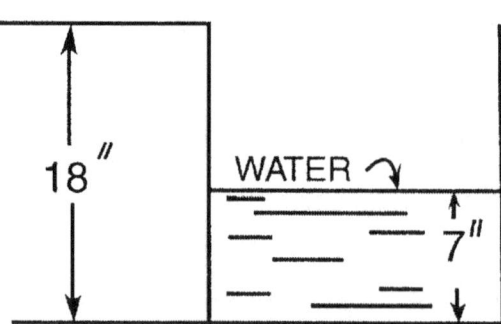

The percentage of the above tank that is filled with water is MOST NEARLY

A. 33   B. 35   C. 37   D. 39

43.____

44.

[TOP VIEW square]

[FRONT VIEW square]

The top and front view of an object are shown above. The right side view will MOST likely look like

A. 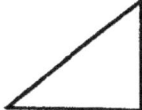   B.    C.    D.

45.

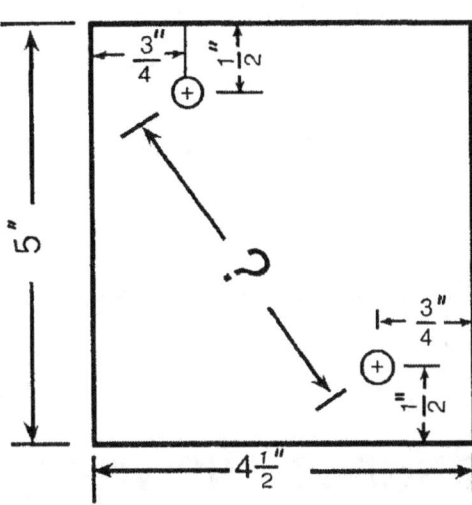

The distance between centers of the holes in the above diagram is MOST NEARLY

A. $4\frac{1}{2}"$ B. 4 3/4"   C. 5"   D. $5\frac{1}{4}"$

Questions 46-48.

DIRECTIONS: Questions 46 through 48, inclusive, are to be answered in accordance with the paragraph below.

A steam heating system with steam having a pressure of less than 10 pounds is called a low-pressure system. The majority of steam-heating systems are of this type. The steam may be provided by low-pressure boilers installed <u>expressly</u> for the purpose, or it may be gener-

ated in boilers at a higher pressure and reduced in pressure before admitted to the heating mains. In other instances, it may be possible to use exhaust steam which has been made to run engines and other machines and which still contains enough heat to be utilized in the heating system. The first case represents the system of heating used in the ordinary residence or other small building; the other two represent the systems of heating employed in industrial buildings where a power plant is installed for general power purposes.

46. According to the above paragraph, whether or not a steam heating system is considered a low pressure system is determined by the pressure

    A. generated by the boiler
    B. in the heating main
    C. at the inlet side of the reducing valve
    D. of the exhaust

47. According to the above paragraph, steam used for heating is sometimes obtained from steam

    A. generated principally to operate machinery
    B. exhausted from larger boilers
    C. generated at low pressure and brought up to high pressure before being used
    D. generated by engines other than boilers

48. As used in the above paragraph, the word *expressly* means

    A. rapidly   B. specifically
    C. usually   D. mainly

49. Of the following words, the one that is CORRECTLY spelled is

    A. suficient   B. sufficant
    C. sufficient   D. suficiant

50. Of the following words, the one that is CORRECTLY spelled is

    A. fairly   B. fairley   C. farely   D. fairlie

KEY (CORRECT ANSWERS)

1. B	11. B	21. C	31. B	41. D
2. A	12. D	22. C	32. A	42. B
3. A	13. D	23. B	33. D	43. D
4. C	14. B	24. A	34. B	44. A
5. C	15. C	25. C	35. D	45. C
6. C	16. C	26. C	36. A	46. B
7. B	17. B	27. B	37. B	47. A
8. A	18. D	28. B	38. B	48. B
9. C	19. B	29. A	39. C	49. C
10. B	20. A	30. B	40. D	50. A

EXAMINATION SECTION
TEST 1

DIRECTIONS: Each question or incomplete statement is followed by several suggested answers or completions. Select the one that BEST answers the question or completes the statement. *PRINT THE LETTER OF THE CORRECT ANSWER IN THE SPACE AT THE RIGHT.*

1. The composition of plumber's solder for wiping is APPROXIMATELY (ratio of tin to lead) 1._____

   A. 40-60 B. 50-50 C. 60-40 D. 70-30

2. A device used to lift sewage to the level of a sewer from a floor below the sewer grade is known as a(n) 2._____

   A. elevator B. ejector C. sump D. conveyer

3. A check valve in a piping system will 3._____

   A. permit excessive pressures in a boiler
   B. eliminate water hammer
   C. permit water to flow in only one direction
   D. control the rate of flow of water

4. The chemical MOST frequently used to clean drains clogged with grease is 4._____

   A. muriatic acid B. soda ash
   C. ammonia D. caustic soda

5. To test for leaks in a newly installed C.I. waste stack, 5._____

   A. oil of peppermint is poured into the top of the stack
   B. smoke under pressure is pumped into the stack
   C. a water meter is used to measure the water flow
   D. dye is placed in the system at the top of the stack

6. When installing a catch basin, the outlet should be located 6._____

   A. at the same level as the inlet
   B. above the inlet
   C. below the inlet
   D. at the invert

7. The copper float in a low down water tank is perforated so that water enters the ball. As a result, the tank will 7._____

   A. flush once, and then will not operate again
   B. not flush at all
   C. not flush completely
   D. continue to flush, but water will be wasted

8. If water leaks from the stem of a faucet when the faucet is opened, the _____ should be 8._____

   A. faucet; replaced B. cap nut; rethreaded
   C. seat; reground D. packing; replaced

29

9. In a hot water heating system, it may be necessary to *bleed* radiators to

   A. relieve high steam pressure
   B. permit entrapped, air to escape
   C. allow condensate to return to the boiler
   D. drain off waste water

10. When painting raw wood, puttying of nail holes should be done

    A. 24 hours before the prime coat
    B. immediately before the prime coat
    C. after the prime coat and before the second coat
    D. after the second coat and before the finish

11. In general, the one of the following that will dry *tack free* in the SHORTEST time is

    A. lacquer   B. varnish   C. enamel   D. oil paint

12. The *vehicle* MOST frequently used in paints for exterior wood surfaces is

    A. white lead   B. linseed oil
    C. japan   D. varnish

13. Painting of an interior plastered wall is usually delayed until the plaster is dry. If this practice is NOT followed, the paint might

    A. chalk   B. fade   C. run   D. blister

14. A *sealer* applied over knots and pitch streaks to prevent *bleeding* through paint is

    A. shellac   B. lacquer
    C. coal tar   D. carnauba wax

15. Painting of outside steel in near freezing (32° F) weather is poor practice MAINLY because

    A. the paint will not dry properly
    B. ice will form in the thinner
    C. more paint is required
    D. paint fumes are dangerous

16. When repainting exterior woodwork that has a glossy finish, good adhesion of paint is BEST obtained by first

    A. *washing* the work with diluted lye
    B. *dulling* the work with sandpaper
    C. *warming* the work with an electric heater
    D. *roughening* the work with a rasp

17. The one of the following methods of cleaning steelwork prior to painting that is NOT commonly used on exterior work, such as bridges, is

    A. sandblasting   B. flame cleaning
    C. wire brushing   D. pickling

18. When spraying oil paints, the type of gun and nozzle preferred is a _____ feed gun, _____ mix nozzle.

    A. pressure; internal
    B. pressure, external
    C. syphon; internal
    D. syphon; external

19. When opening a bag of cement, you find that the cement is lumpy.
    The cement should be

    A. discarded and not used at all
    B. crushed before placing in the mixer
    C. used as is since the mixer will grind it
    D. well mixed with water and stored overnight before using

20. A 1:2:4 concrete mix by volume is specified.
    If 6 cubic feet of cement is to be used in the mix, the volume of sand to use is, in cubic feet,

    A. 3   B. 6   C. 12   D. 24

21. Honeycombing in concrete is BEST prevented by

    A. increasing water-cement ratio
    B. heating concrete in cold weather
    C. using mechanical vibrators
    D. adding calcium chloride

22. When a lightweight concrete is required, the one of the following that is COMMONLY used as an aggregate is

    A. gravel   B. brick chips   C. stone   D. cinders

23. A rubbed finish on concrete is USUALLY obtained by use of a

    A. carborundum brick
    B. garnet sanding belt
    C. fibre brush and wax
    D. pad of steel wool

24. A copper strip is frequently embedded in the concrete across a construction joint in a concrete wall.
    The purpose of this is to

    A. make a watertight joint
    B. bond the two parts of the wall together
    C. prevent unequal settlement
    D. retard temperature cracking

25. In brickwork laid in common bond, a header course USUALLY occurs in every _____ course.

    A. 2nd   B. 4th   C. 6th   D. 8th

26. Pointing of brickwork refers to

    A. cutting brick to fit
    B. patching mortar joints
    C. attaching brick veneer
    D. arranging brick in an arch

27. Furring is applied to brick walls to

   A. strengthen the wall
   B. waterproof the wall
   C. provide ventilation to prevent condensation
   D. provide a base for lathing

28. The FIRST coat in plaster work is *scratched* in order to

   A. remove excess plaster
   B. smooth the base for the second coat
   C. provide a bond for the second coat
   D. strengthen the base coat

29. An alloy used where resistance to corrosion is important is

   A. tungsten   B. mild steel   C. monel   D. tin

30. The size of iron pipe is given in terms of its nominal

   A. weight   B. inside diameter
   C. outside diameter   D. wall thickness

31. When preparing surfaces to be soldered, the FIRST step is

   A. tinning   B. sweating   C. heating   D. cleaning

32. To test for leaks in an acetylene torch, it is BEST that one use

   A. soapy water   B. a match
   C. a gas with a strong odor D. a pressure gauge

33. One advantage of using a Pittsburgh lock seam when joining two pieces of sheet metal is that, once formed in the shop, it may be assembled anywhere with a

   A. hickey   B. swage   C. template   D. mallet

34. White cast iron is

   A. hard and brittle   B. hard and ductile
   C. ductile and malleable   D. brittle and malleable

35. The gage used for measuring copper wire is

   A. U.S. Standard   B. Stubbs
   C. Washburn and Moen   D. Brown and Sharpe

36. The BEST flux to use when soldering copper wires in an electric circuit is

   A. sal ammoniac   B. zinc chloride
   C. rosin   D. borax

37. The spark test, to determine the approximate composition of an unknown metal, is made by

   A. holding the metal against a grinding wheel
   B. striking flint on the unknown metal
   C. connecting wires from a source of electric power to the metal and striking an arc with a bare wire
   D. heating with an oxyacetylene torch

38. The one of the following metals that is MOST commonly used for bearings is

    A. duraluminum B. brass C. babbit D. lead

39. A *tailstock* is found on a

    A. drill press B. shaper C. planer D. lathe

40. The BEST lubricant to use when cutting screw threads in steel is

    A. naphtha
    C. lard oil
    B. 3-in-1 oil
    D. linseed oil

41. When a high speed cutting tool is required, the tip is frequently made of

    A. carborundum
    C. bronze
    B. tungsten carbide
    D. vanadium

42. A nut is turned on a 3/4"-10 bolt.
    When the nut is turned five complete turns on this bolt, the distance it moves along the bolt

    A. depends on the type of thread
    C. is 0.375 inches
    B. is 0.2 inches
    D. is 0.5 inches

43. Of the following, the STRONGEST screw thread form is the

    A. Whitworth
    C. National Standard
    B. Acme
    D. V

44. *Knurling* refers to

    A. rolling depressions in a fixed pattern on a cylindrical surface
    B. turning between centers on a lathe
    C. making deep cuts in a flat plate with a milling machine
    D. drilling matching holes in bolt and nut for a cotter pin

45. A special device used to guide the drill as well as to hold the work when drilling is known as a

    A. dolly B. jig C. chuck D. collet

46. Tools that have a *Morse taper* would be used on a

    A. milling machine
    C. planer
    B. shaper
    D. drill press

47. When tapping a blind hole in a plate, the FIRST tap to use is a

    A. plug B. bottoming C. lead D. taper

48. An important safety practice to remember when cutting a rivet with a chisel is to wear

    A. leather gloves
    C. cup goggles
    B. steel toe shoes
    D. a hard hat

49. Electricians working around *live wires* should wear gloves made of

  A. asbestos   B. metal mesh   C. leather   D. rubber

50. Storage of oily rags presents a safety hazard because of possible

  A. fire
  C. attraction of rats
  B. poisonous flames
  D. leakage of oil

KEY (CORRECT ANSWERS)

1. A	11. A	21. C	31. D	41. B
2. B	12. B	22. D	32. A	42. D
3. C	13. D	23. A	33. D	43. B
4. D	14. A	24. A	34. A	44. A
5. B	15. A	25. C	35. B	45. B
6. C	16. B	26. B	36. C	46. D
7. D	17. D	27. D	37. A	47. D
8. D	18. A	28. C	38. C	48. C
9. B	19. A	29. C	39. D	49. D
10. C	20. C	30. B	40. C	50. A

TEST 2

DIRECTIONS: Each question or incomplete statement is followed by several suggested answers or completions. Select the one that BEST answers the question or completes the statement. *PRINT THE LETTER OF THE CORRECT ANSWER IN THE SPACE AT THE RIGHT.*

1. *Shimmying* of the front wheels of a truck is MOST frequently caused by 1.____

    A. worn front brake drums
    B. a worn differential gear
    C. a loose steering gear
    D. a dead shock absorber

2. The MOST important reason for maintaining correct air pressure in all tires of a truck is to 2.____

    A. prevent the truck from swerving when brakes are applied
    B. permit the truck to stop quicker in an emergency
    C. provide a smoother ride
    D. prevent excessive wear on the tires

3. The oil gage on the dashboard of a truck indicates 3.____

    A. the amount of oil in the pan
    B. the pressure at which the oil is being pumped
    C. if the oil filter is working
    D. the temperature of the oil in the motor

4. An unbalanced wheel on a truck is corrected by 4.____

    A. bending the rim slightly
    B. adjusting the king pin
    C. changing the ratio of caster to camber
    D. adding small weights to the rim

5. A cold motor on a truck should be warmed up in wintertime by 5.____

    A. turning on the heater and pouring warm water into the radiator
    B. allowing the motor to idle for a few minutes
    C. racing the motor
    D. alternately pressing the gas pedal to the floor and releasing it

6. The brake pedal on a truck goes to the floorboard when pushed. 6.____
   The one of the following that would cause this condition is

    A. air in the hydraulic system
    B. wet brakes
    C. excessive fluid in the cylinders
    D. a loose backing plate

7. The ammeter of a truck indicates no charge during operation even though the battery is 7.____
   run down. To find the fault, the generator field terminal is grounded. The ammeter now shows a charge. The part that is defective is the

    A. generator field coil
    B. armature
    C. brushes
    D. voltage regulator

8. The part used to control the ratio of air and gasoline in a truck engine is the

   A. bogie B. filter C. carburetor D. pump

9. The MAIN purpose of a vacuum booster on a truck engine is to

   A. increase the manifold vacuum
   B. assist windshield wiper operation
   C. provide a steadier fuel flow
   D. govern engine speed

10. The purpose of grounding the frame of an electric motor is to

    A. prevent excessive vibration
    B. eliminate shock hazards
    C. reduce power requirements
    D. prevent overheating

11. The one of the following that is NOT part of an electric motor is a

    A. brush B. rheostat C. pole D. commutator

12. An electrical transformer would be used to

    A. change current from AC to DC
    B. raise or lower the power
    C. raise or lower the voltage
    D. change the frequency

13. The piece of equipment that would be rated in ampere hours is a

    A. storage battery
    B. bus bar
    C. rectifier
    D. capacitor

14. A ballast is a necessity in a(n)

    A. motor generator set
    B. fluorescent lighting system
    C. oil circuit breaker
    D. synchronous converter

15. The power factor in an AC circuit is on when

    A. no current is flowing
    B. the voltage at the source is a minimum
    C. the voltage and current are in phase
    D. there is no load

16.

    Neglecting the internal resistance in the battery, the current flowing through the battery shown in the sketch above is _____ amp.

    A. 3 B. 6 C. 9 D. 12

17. When excess current flows, a circuit breaker is opened directly by the action of a 17.____

    A. condenser   B. transistor   C. relay   D. solenoid

18. The MAIN purpose of bridging in building floor construction is to 18.____

    A. spread floor loads evenly to joists
    B. reduce the number of joists required
    C. permit use of thinner subflooring
    D. reduce noise passage through floors

19. Of the following, the material MOST commonly used for subflooring is 19.____

    A. rock lath   B. insulation board
    C. plywood   D. transite

20. In connection with stair construction, the one of the following that is LEAST related to the others is 20.____

    A. tread   B. cap   C. nosing   D. riser

21. The type of nail MOST commonly used in flooring is 21.____

    A. common   B. cut   C. brad   D. casing

22. The edge joint of flooring boards is COMMONLY 22.____

    A. mortise and tenon   B. shiplap
    C. half lap   D. tongue and groove

23. The purpose of a ridge board in building construction is to 23.____

    A. locate corners of a building
    B. keep plaster work smooth
    C. support the ends of roof rafters
    D. conceal openings at the eaves

24. To prevent splintering of wood when using an auger bit, 24.____

    A. the bit should be hollow ground
    B. hold the piece of wood in a vise
    C. clamp a piece of scrap wood to the back of the piece being drilled
    D. use a slow speed on the drill press

25. End grain of a post can be MOST easily planed by use of a _____ plane. 25.____

    A. rafter   B. jack   C. fore   D. block

26. A butt gauge is used when 26.____

    A. hanging doors   B. laying out stairs
    C. making rafter cuts   D. framing studs

27. The one of the following grades of sandpaper with the FINEST grit is 27.____

    A. 0   B. 2/0   C. 1/2   D. 1

28. The sum of the following numbers, 3 7/8, 14 1/4, 6 7/16, 22 3/16, 8 1/2 is   28.____

    A. 55 1/16   B. 55 1/8   C. 55 3/16   D. 55 1/4

29. The area of the rectangular field shown in the diagram at the right is, in square feet,   29.____
    A. 29,456
    B. 29,626
    C. 29,716
    D. 29,836

(Diagram: rectangle labeled 437 FT. on top and 68 ft on the side)

30. The cost of material is approximately 3/8ths of the total cost of a certain job. If the total cost of the job is $127.56, then the cost of material is MOST NEARLY   30.____

    A. $47.83   B. $48.24   C. $48.65   D. $49.06

31. A blueprint is drawn to a scale of 1/4" = 1'0". A line on the blueprint that is not dimensioned is measured with a ruler and found to be 3 3/8" long.
The length represented by this line is   31.____

    A. 13'2"   B. 13'4"   C. 13'6"   D. 13'8"

32. A maintainer, in repairing a brick wall, spends one-half hour getting materials, forty-three minutes chipping and cleaning the wall, fifteen minutes mixing the mortar, and one hour and twenty-seven minutes in applying the brick and finishing.
The total time spent on this repair job is _____ hours _____ minute(s).   32.____

    A. 2; 45   B. 2; 50   C. 2; 55   D. 3; 0

33. *Employees are responsible for the good care, proper maintenance, and serviceable condition of property issued or assigned to their use.*
As used above, *serviceable condition* means MOST NEARLY   33.____

    A. capable of being repaired   B. fit for use
    C. ease of handling   D. minimum cost

34. An employee shall be on the alert constantly for potential accident hazards.
As used above, *potential* means MOST NEARLY   34.____

    A. dangerous   B. careless   C. possible   D. frequent

Questions 35-37.

DIRECTIONS: Questions 35 to 37, inclusive, are to be answered in accordance with the following paragraph.

All cement work contracts, more or less, in setting. The contraction in concrete walls and other structures causes fine cracks to develop at regular intervals. The tendency to contract increases in direct proportion to the quantity of cement in the concrete. A rich mixture will contract more than a lean mixture. A concrete wall, which has been made of a very lean mixture and which has been built by filling only about one foot in depth of concrete in the form each day will frequently require close inspection to reveal the cracks.

35. According to the above paragraph,

    A. shrinkage seldom occurs in concrete
    B. shrinkage occurs only in certain types of concrete
    C. by placing concrete at regular intervals, shrinkage may be avoided
    D. it is impossible to prevent shrinkage

36. According to the above paragraph, the one of the factors which reduces shrinkage in concrete is the

    A. volume of concrete in wall
    B. height of each day's pour
    C. length of wall
    D. length and height of wall

37. According to the above paragraph, a rich mixture

    A. pours the easiest
    B. shows the largest amount of cracks
    C. is low in cement content
    D. need not be inspected since cracks are few

Questions 38-39.

DIRECTIONS: Questions 38 and 39 are to be answered in accordance with the following paragraph.

Painting is done to preserve surfaces, and unless the surface is properly prepared, good preservation will not be possible. Apply paint only to clean dry surfaces. After a surface has been scaled, which means that all loose paint and rust are removed by chipping, scraping, and wire brushing, be sure all dust and dirt are completely removed.

38. According to the above paragraph, the MAIN purpose of painting a wall is to _____ the wall.

    A. clean
    B. waterproof
    C. protect
    D. remove dust from

39. According to the above paragraph,

    A. chipping, scraping, and wire brushing are the only methods permitted for cleaning surfaces
    B. painting is effective only when the surface is clean
    C. scaling refers only to the removal of rust
    D. paint may be applied on wet surfaces

40. The order in which the dimensions of stock are listed on a bill of materials is

    A. thickness, length, and width
    B. thickness, width, and length
    C. width, length, and thickness
    D. length, thickness, and width

41. The glue that will BEST withstand extreme exposure to moisture and water is _____ glue.

    A. polyvinyl
    B. resorcinol
    C. powdered resin
    D. protein

42. Four board feet of lumber, listed at $350.00 per M, will cost

    A. $3.50   B. $1.40   C. $1.30   D. $4.00

43. The cap iron or chip breaker stiffens the plane iron and

    A. protects the cutting edge
    B. curls the shaving
    C. regulates the thickness of the shaving
    D. reduces mouth gap

44. Coping-saw blades have teeth shaped like those on a _____ saw.

    A. dovetail   B. crosscut   C. back   D. rip

45. Of the following, the claw hammer that is BEST suited for general use in a woodworking shop is the _____ claw.

    A. straight
    B. bell-faced curved
    C. plain-faced curved
    D. adze eye curved

46. The natural binder which cements wood fibers together and makes wood solid is

    A. cellulose
    B. lignin
    C. alpha-cellulose
    D. trichocarpa

47. The plane that is BEST suited for trimming the bottom of a dado or lap joint is the _____ plane.

    A. block   B. router   C. rabbet   D. core-box

48. Brads are fasteners that are similar to _____ nails.

    A. escutcheon
    B. box
    C. finishing
    D. duplex head

49. The plane in which the plane iron is inserted with its bevel in the up position is the _____ plane.

    A. fore   B. rabbet   C. block   D. circular

50. Coating materials used to protect wood against fire USUALLY contain a water soluble fire-retardant such as

    A. ammonium chloride
    B. sodium perborate
    C. sodium silicate
    D. sal soda

KEY (CORRECT ANSWERS)

1. C	11. B	21. B	31. C	41. B
2. D	12. C	22. D	32. C	42. B
3. B	13. A	23. C	33. B	43. B
4. D	14. B	24. C	34. C	44. D
5. B	15. C	25. D	35. D	45. B
6. A	16. A	26. A	36. B	46. B
7. D	17. D	27. B	37. B	47. B
8. C	18. A	28. D	38. C	48. C
9. B	19. C	29. C	39. B	49. C
10. B	20. B	30. A	40. B	50. C

EXAMINATION SECTION
TEST 1

DIRECTIONS: Each question or incomplete statement is followed by several suggested answers or completions. Select the one that BEST answers the question or completes the statement. *PRINT THE LETTER OF THE CORRECT ANSWER IN THE SPACE AT THE RIGHT.*

1. On an engine lathe, the saddle is a part which

    A. is attached to the tailstock
    B. rotates and holds the faceplate
    C. slides along the ways
    D. houses the back gears

2. To facilitate milling cast iron, it is BEST to use

    A. an emulsion of soluble oil and water as a lubricant
    B. an emulsion of soluble oil and water with a small percentage of soda as a lubricant
    C. lard oil as a lubricant
    D. no lubricant

3. When using a milling machine in a machine shop, a MAJOR difference of climb milling as compared to standard milling is that climb milling

    A. uses more power
    B. produces a better finish
    C. uses a downward cut
    D. uses cutters with less rake

4. In an automotive gasoline engine, the camshaft is used PRIMARILY to

    A. drive the transmission
    B. operate the valve lifters
    C. change the reciprocating motion of the pistons to rotary motion
    D. operate the choke mechanism

5. A magnetic motor starter is to be controlled with momentary start-stop pushbuttons at two locations.
   The number of control wires required, respectively, in the conduit between the controller and the first station and in the conduit between the two stations is _____ and _____.

    A. 3;3   B. 4; 4   C. 3; 4   D. 2; 4

6. The type of fitting to use to join a 1 inch branch compressed air, pipe line to a 2 inch main air line is a

    A. reducing valve   B. reducing coupling
    C. reducing tee   D. street elbow

7. If steel weighs 0.30 pounds per cubic inch, then the weight of a 2 inch square steel bar 90 inches long is _____ pounds.

    A. 27   B. 54   C. 108   D. 360

8. In arc welding, the filler metal is provided PRIMARILY by

   A. the metal to be welded
   B. a second rod of filler metal
   C. the slag
   D. the electrode

9. Oil or grease should NOT be applied to the oxygen valve of an oxyacetylene torch PRIMARILY because this can

   A. produce an explosion hazard
   B. corrode the valve
   C. give an incorrect pressure reading
   D. make the valve too slippery to handle

10. The PRIMARY function of the thermostat in the cooling system of an automobile engine is to

    A. control the operating temperature of the engine
    B. keep the operating temperature of the engine as low as possible
    C. provide the proper amount of heat for the heater
    D. retain engine heat when the engine gets hot

11. The PRIMARY purpose of the condenser in the ignition circuit of a gasoline engine is to

    A. boost the ignition voltage
    B. rectify the ignition voltage
    C. adjust the coil voltage
    D. reduce arcing at the distributor breaker points

12. The PRIMARY purpose of the differential in the rear drive train of an automotive vehicle is to allow each of the rear wheels to

    A. rotate at different speeds
    B. go in reverse
    C. rotate with maximum torque
    D. absorb road shocks

13. When grinding a fillet weld smooth, it is best NOT to grind

    A. after the weld has cooled off
    B. slowly
    C. too much of the weld material away
    D. the surface smooth

14. When using a hand file to finish a round piece of wood rod held between lathe centers, it is usually BEST to

    A. hold the file handle with one hand and to guide the file with the other hand
    B. use the file with the lathe not rotating
    C. hold the file with one hand and guide the workpiece with the other hand
    D. use a file without a handle

15. If the voltage on a 3-phase squirrel case induction motor is reduced to 90% of its rating, the starting current

    A. increases slightly
    B. is unchanged
    C. decreases 10%
    D. decreases 20%

16. If the voltage on a 3-phase squirrel case induction motor is reduced to 90% of its rating, the full load current

    A. decreases slightly
    B. is unchanged
    C. increases 10%
    D. increases 20%

17. When laying brick, the PRIMARY reason for wetting the brick before laying it is that

    A. the brick will absorb less water from the mortar and form a better bond
    B. wet bricks are easier to position
    C. wet bricks take less time to form a bond to mortar
    D. less cement is needed in the mortar

18. Concrete is a mixture that NORMALLY consists of cement,

    A. sand, and water
    B. sand, mortar, and water
    C. gravel, and water
    D. sand, gravel, and water

19. A type of rivet which can be put in place even when a worker does NOT have access to the back side of the work is known as a _____ rivet.

    A. *bucking*
    B. *double-head*
    C. *pop*
    D. *side*

20. The fraction which is equal to 0.875 is

    A. 7/16
    B. 5/8
    C. 3/4
    D. 7/8

21. When fabricating forms for pouring concrete, the MAIN advantage of using plywood sheets over sheets made of pine boards is that plywood

    A. doesn't splinter
    B. is lighter
    C. is less expensive
    D. resists warping better

22. When chipping concrete with a pneumatic hammer, the MOST important safety item that a man should wear is

    A. goggles
    B. gloves
    C. a hard hat
    D. rubber boots

23. It is considered POOR practice to paint a wooden ladder PRIMARILY because the

    A. paint will wear off in time
    B. rails will become susceptible to damage
    C. paint will shorten the life of the rungs
    D. paint can hide serious defects

24. A concrete wall is 36' long, 9' high, and 1 1/2' thick. The number of cubic yards of concrete that were needed to make this wall is

    A. 14
    B. 18
    C. 27
    D. 36

25. Before disassembling a complex mechanical machine, a mechanic may use a center punch to make adjacent punch marks on two or more of the parts in the machine in order to

    A. mark each part as he removes it
    B. check the hardness of the parts
    C. loosen the parts
    D. give himself a guide for correct reassembly

26. From among the following tools, the BEST one to use in cutting off a section of 4-inch cast iron pipe would be a

    A. hammer and chisel   B. pneumatic hammer
    C. hammer and star drill   D. hacksaw

27. The MOST important reason for removing pressure from an air hose before breaking a hose connection is to avoid

    A. damage to the air compressor
    B. losing air
    C. damage to the hose connection
    D. personal injury

28. When using a rope fall to lower a heavy load vertically, the strain on the hand line can be reduced and the load lowered more safely if the

    A. rope is wound three or four times around a fixed post
    B. rope is lightly greased
    C. rope is held very tightly in the sheaves of the fall
    D. sheaves of the fall are small in diameter

29. Oil is frequently applied to the inside of forms prior to pouring concrete in them in order to

    A. make the concrete flow better
    B. make stripping easier
    C. keep the moisture in the concrete
    D. protect the forms

30. The instrument generally used to determine the specific gravity of a lead-acid storage battery is the

    A. ammeter   B. voltmeter   C. ohmmeter   D. hydrometer

31. A tachometer is an instrument that is used to measure

    A. horizontal distances
    B. radial distances
    C. current in electric circuits
    D. motor speed

32. If the centers of a lathe are out of line when turning a cylindrical piece, it will cause

    A. the centers to be damaged
    B. a spiral groove to be cut on the piece

C. the cutting tool to be damaged
D. the piece to have a taper

33. A low reading on the oil pressure gauge of a gasoline engine may mean that the

    A. engine bearings are too tight
    B. crankcase oil level is too low
    C. transmission oil level is too low
    D. transmission oil needs changing

34. Although cloth tapes are used for taking measurements in many kinds of work, they should NOT be used when taking accurate measurements PRIMARILY because

    A. small changes in the amount of pull on these tapes can make a big difference in the reading
    B. the numbers become worn easily and are thus difficult to read
    C. small temperature changes cause large changes in readings
    D. there are too few subdivisions of each inch on these tapes

35. When painting walls with two coats of paint, a different color is used for each coat PRIMARILY to

    A. check for full coverage by the second coat
    B. provide a better appearance
    C. lower the painting cost
    D. allow the painter to use any color paint for the first coat

36. To drill a hole in the same place on a number of identical steel parts, it is BEST to use a

    A. blanking tool   B. punch press
    C. counterbore   D. jig

37. The MAIN purpose of a chuck on a lathe is to

    A. hold the workpiece
    B. hold the cutting tool
    C. allow speed changes to be made
    D. allow screw threads to be turned

38. The metal which has the GREATEST resistance to the flow of electricity is

    A. steel   B. copper   C. silver   D. gold

39. Tinning a soldering iron means

    A. applying flux to the tip
    B. cleaning the tip to make it bright
    C. applying a coat of solder to the tip
    D. heating the iron to the proper temperature

40. A protractor is an instrument that is used to

    A. measure the thickness of shims
    B. drill blind holes
    C. measure angles
    D. drill tapped holes

KEY (CORRECT ANSWERS)

1. C	11. D	21. D	31. D
2. D	12. A	22. A	32. D
3. C	13. C	23. D	33. B
4. B	14. A	24. B	34. A
5. C	15. C	25. D	35. A
6. C	16. C	26. A	36. D
7. C	17. A	27. D	37. A
8. D	18. D	28. A	38. A
9. A	19. C	29. B	39. C
10. A	20. D	30. D	40. C

TEST 2

DIRECTIONS: Each question or incomplete statement is followed by several suggested answers or completions. Select the one that BEST answers the question or completes the statement. *PRINT THE LETTER OF THE CORRECT ANSWER IN THE SPACE AT THE RIGHT.*

1. Common nail sizes are designated by

   A. penny size
   B. weight
   C. head size
   D. shank diameter

2. Toggle bolts should be used to fasten conduit clamps to a _____ wall.

   A. concrete
   B. hollow tile
   C. brick
   D. solid masonry

3. Backlash in a pair of meshed gears is defined as the

   A. distance between the gear centers
   B. gear ratio of the pair
   C. wear of the teeth
   D. *play* between the gear teeth

4. Relief valves on an air supply reservoir are used for the purpose of

   A. protecting the reservoir against excessively high pressures
   B. compensating for air leakage from the reservoir
   C. retaining the air in the reservoir
   D. draining moisture from the reservoir

5. Of the following, the BEST tool to use for securely tightening a one-inch standard hexagonal nut is a(n)

   A. monkey wrench
   B. open-end wrench
   C. Stillson wrench
   D. pair of heavy duty pliers

6. The type of pipe which is MOST likely to be broken by careless handling is one made of

   A. copper   B. steel   C. brass   D. cast iron

7. Open-end wrenches are usually made with the sides of the jaws at about a 15 degree angle to the centerline of the handle.
   The PURPOSE of this type of design is that it

   A. increases the leverage of the wrench
   B. enables the wrench to lock on to the bolt head
   C. is useful when using the wrench in close quarters
   D. prevents extending the handle with a piece of pipe

8. The type of tool which is used with a portable electric drill to cut 2-inch diameter circular holes in wood is the

   A. reamer
   B. twist drill
   C. hole saw
   D. circular saw

49

9. For a certain job, you will need 25 steel bars 1 inch in diameter and 4'6" long. If these bars weigh 3 pounds per foot of length, then the TOTAL weight for all 25 bars is _____ pounds.

   A. 13.5   B. 75.0   C. 112.5   D. 337.5

10. If the allowable load on a wooden scaffold is 60 pounds per square foot and the scaffold surface area is 3 feet by 12 feet, then the MAXIMUM total distributed load that is permitted on the scaffold is _____ pounds.

    A. 720   B. 1800   C. 2160   D. 2400

11. If the floor area of one shop is 15' by 21'3" and the size of an adjacent shop is 18' by 30'6", then the TOTAL floor area of these two shops is _____ square feet.

    A. 1127.75   B. 867.75   C. 549.0   D. 318.75

12. To make certain that two points separated by a vertical distance of 8 feet are in exact vertical alignment, it would be BEST to use a

    A. plumb bob
    B. spirit level
    C. protractor
    D. mason's line

13. An offset screwdriver is MOST useful for turning a wood screw when

    A. the screw is large
    B. space above the screw is limited
    C. the screw is the Phillips type
    D. the screw must be tightened very securely

14. If an 8-32 x 1 1" machine screw is not available, the screw which could MOST easily be modified to use in an emergency is the

    A. 8-36 x 1"
    B. 10-32 x 1"
    C. 6-32 x 1 1/2"
    D. 8-32 x 1 1/2"

15. After a file has been used on soft material, the BEST way to clean the file is to use

    A. a file card
    B. fine emery cloth
    C. a bench brush
    D. a cleaning solution

16. The type of wrench that should be used to tighten a nut or bolt to a specified number of foot-pounds is a _____ wrench.

    A. torque   B. spanner   C. box   D. lug

17. When a hacksaw blade is turned at right angles to its holding frame, it is done PRIMARILY to

    A. increase the accuracy of cutting
    B. reduce the strain on the frame
    C. cut more rapidly
    D. make cuts which are deeper than the frame

18. The PRIMARY purpose of galvanizing steel is to

    A. increase the strength of the steel
    B. provide a good base for painting

C. prevent rusting of the steel
D. improve the appearance of the steel

19. When installing a heavy new machine in a shop, the BEST way to level the machine on the shop floor is to

   A. use steel shims under the feet
   B. use a thin layer of cement under the feet
   C. grind the feet of the machine to suit
   D. install adjustable shock mounts

20. The type of valve that permits fluid to flow in one direction ONLY in a pipe run is a _____ valve.

   A. check   B. gate   C. globe   D. cross

21. If the scale on a shop drawing is 1/2 inch to the foot, then the length of a part which measures 4 1/4 inches long on the drawing has a length of APPROXIMATELY _____ feet.

   A. 2 1/8   B. 4 1/4   C. 8 1/2   D. 10 3/4

22. It is important to use safety shoes PRIMARILY to guard the feet against

   A. tripping hazards   B. heavy falling objects
   C. shock hazards   D. mud and dirt

23. When using a wrench to tighten a bolt, it is considered BAD practice to extend the handle of the wrench with a pipe for added leverage PRIMARILY because

   A. the pipe may break
   B. the bolt head may be broken off
   C. more space will be needed to turn the wrench with the pipe on it
   D. no increase in leverage is obtained in this manner

24. To accurately measure the small gap between relay contacts, it is BEST to use a(n)

   A. depth gauge   B. GO-NO GO gauge
   C. feeler gauge   D. inside caliper

25. The plumbing symbol shown on the right represents a
   A. steam trap
   B. coupling
   C. cross fitting
   D. valve

26. On oxyacetylene welding equipment, the feed pressure of the gases is reduced by means of

   A. tip valves   B. regulator valves
   C. relief valves   D. nozzle size

27. The purpose of the ignition coil in a gasoline engine is PRIMARILY to

   A. smooth the voltage   B. raise the voltage
   C. raise the current   D. smooth the current

28. The weight per foot of length of a 2" x 2" square steel bar as compared to a 1" x 1" square steel bar is _____ times as much.

    A. two   B. four   C. six   D. eight

29. Electric arc welding is COMMONLY done using _____ amperage and _____ voltage.

    A. low; low   B. low; high
    C. high; low   D. high; high

30. Creosote is COMMONLY used

    A. to preserve wood
    B. to produce a good finish on wood
    C. as a primer coat of paint on wood
    D. to fireproof wood

31. The term *shipping* when applied to rope means

    A. coiling the rope in a tight ball
    B. lubricating the strands with tallow
    C. wetting the rope with water to make it easier to coil
    D. binding the ends with cord to prevent unraveling

32. Many portable electric power tools, such as electric drills, which operate on 110V A.C., have a third conductor in the power cord.
The reason for this extra conductor is to

    A. prevent overheating of the power cord
    B. provide a spare conductor
    C. make the power cord stronger
    D. ground the case of the tool

33. The sum of 4 feet 3 1/4 inches, 7 feet 2 1/2 inches, and 11 feet 1/4 inch is _____ feet _____ inches.

    A. 21; 6 1/4   B. 22; 6   C. 23; 5   D. 24; 5 3/4

34. The number 0.038 is read as

    A. 38 tenths   B. 38 hundredths
    C. 38 thousandths   D. 38 ten-thousandths

35. Assume that an employee is paid at the rate of $5.43 per hour with time and a half for overtime past 40 hours in a week.
If he works 43 hours in a week, his gross weekly pay is

    A. $217.20   B. $219.20   C. $229.59   D. $241.64

36. Vapor lock in a vehicle with a gasoline engine is caused by excessive heat.
To prevent vapor lock, it may be necessary to relocate the(a)

    A. ignition system   B. cooling system
    C. starter motor   D. part of the fuel line

37. An ohmmeter is an instrument for measuring electrical

    A. voltage   B. current   C. power   D. resistance

38. A thermal overload device on a motor is used to protect it against

    A. high voltage
    B. over-speeding
    C. excessively high current
    D. low temperatures

39. A union is a pipe fitting that is used to join together

    A. two pipes of different diameters
    B. two pipes of the same diameter
    C. a threaded pipe to a sweated pipe
    D. two sweated pipes of the same diameter

40. If a 30 ampere fuse is placed in a fuse box for a circuit requiring a 15 ampere fuse,

    A. serious damage to the circuit may result from an overload
    B. better protection will be provided for the circuit
    C. the larger fuse will tend to blow more often since it carries more current
    D. it will eliminate maintenance problems

KEY (CORRECT ANSWERS)

1. A	11. B	21. C	31. D
2. B	12. A	22. B	32. D
3. D	13. B	23. B	33. B
4. A	14. D	24. C	34. C
5. B	15. A	25. D	35. D
6. D	16. A	26. B	36. D
7. C	17. D	27. B	37. D
8. C	18. C	28. B	38. C
9. D	19. A	29. C	39. B
10. C	20. A	30. A	40. A

EXAMINATION SECTION
TEST 1

DIRECTIONS: Each question or incomplete statement is followed by several suggested answers or completions. Select the one that BEST answers the question or completes the statement. *PRINT THE LETTER OF THE CORRECT ANSWER IN THE SPACE AT THE RIGHT.*

1. Of the following, the one that is a grease fitting is a _____ fitting. 1._____

   A. Morse
   B. Brown and Sharpe
   C. Zerk
   D. Caliper

2. In an automobile equipped with an ammeter, the ammeter is used to 2._____

   A. indicate current flow
   B. regulate current flow
   C. act as a circuit breaker
   D. measure engine r.p.m.

3. The ignition points in the distributor of a gasoline engine are opened by means of a 3._____

   A. spring
   B. vacuum
   C. cam with lobes
   D. gear

4. MOST automobile engines that use gasoline as fuel operate as _____ cycle engines. 4._____

   A. single
   B. single stroke, single
   C. two-stroke, two-
   D. four-stroke, two-

5. When making a hole in a concrete floor for a machine hold-down bolt, the BEST tool to use is a 5._____

   A. star drill
   B. drift punch
   C. cold chisel
   D. counterboring tool

6. When cutting a hole through a 1/2-inch thick wooden partition, the BEST type of saw to use from among the following choices is a _____ saw. 6._____

   A. coping   B. back   C. rip   D. saber

7. An anodized finish is USUALLY associated with 7._____

   A. aluminum
   B. steel
   C. cast iron
   D. brass

8. Certain devices are used to transmit power from one shaft to another. A device that does so WITHOUT the use of friction is a 8._____

   A. square jaw clutch
   B. simple disk clutch
   C. compression coupling
   D. thermocouple

9. If it is necessary to check the true temperature setting of a thermostat for a shop unit heater, it would be BEST to use 9._____

   A. a mercury thermometer near the heater
   B. a mercury thermometer near the thermostat

55

C. another similar thermostat near the thermostat to be tested
D. a standard thermostat

10. To remove a shrink-fitted collar from a shaft, it would be EASIEST to drive out the shaft after

    A. *chilling* the collar and heating the shaft
    B. *chilling* only the collar
    C. *heating* only the collar
    D. *heating* both the collar and the shaft

11. When drilling a hole in a broken machine stud in order to remove the stud with an extractor, it is BEST to drill the hole

    A. off-center
    B. in the center
    C. with the smallest diameter drill possible
    D. with a taper

12. When fitting two steel parts together, steel dowel pins are GENERALLY used to

    A. keep the parts securely fastened together
    B. provide a wide tolerance fit
    C. provide an adjustable clearance space between the two parts
    D. secure exact placement of these parts with respect to each other

13. When storing files, it is important that they do not touch each other. The PRIMARY reason for this is to prevent

    A. damage to the handles
    B. dirt from collecting in the teeth
    C. damage to the teeth
    D. rusting

14. The frequency of lubrication of bearings and other moving parts of machinery depends PRIMARILY on

    A. the amount of their use   B. their size
    C. the direction of motion   D. the operator's judgment

15. To determine whether the surface of a work bench is horizontal, the BEST tool to use is a

    A. surface gage   B. plumb bob
    C. feeler gage   D. spirit level

16. The swing on a lathe refers to the

    A. distance between centers of the head and tail spindles
    B. size of the face plate
    C. speed range of the gears in r.p.m.
    D. diameter of the largest workpiece that can be turned

17. When installing new piston rings in an air compressor, the piston ring gap is BEST measured by using a(n) 17.____

    A. outside caliper
    B. feeler gage
    C. depth gage
    D. inside caliper

18. When cutting external threads on a pipe, the tool that ACTUALLY cuts the thread is called a 18.____

    A. tap   B. die   C. reamer   D. hone

19. A dynamometer would be MOST useful in 19.____

    A. measuring angles on a steel plate
    B. determining the operating efficiency of an engine
    C. pumping hot fluids out of a tank
    D. heating large shop areas

20. A screw-thread micrometer is used PRIMARILY to measure 20.____

    A. pitch diameter
    B. thread height
    C. major diameter
    D. thread lead

21. A compound-pressure gage found on certain types of equipment is used to indicate 21.____

    A. the sum of two pressures
    B. the difference between two pressures
    C. either vacuum or pressure
    D. two different pressures simultaneously

22. Of the following, the machine screw having the SMALLEST diameter is 22.____

    A. 6-32 x 11/2"
    B. 8-32 x 3/4"
    C. 10-24 x 1"
    D. 12-24 x 1/2"

23. A good quality precision compression spring would MOST probably have 23.____

    A. a small diameter and small wire size
    B. its ends ground flat
    C. a large diameter and large wire size
    D. a high spring rate

24. From among the following materials, the MOST fireproof one for use in maintenance work is 24.____

    A. canvas   B. nylon   C. cotton   D. asbestos

25. The metal which has the GREATEST tendency to crack when dropped onto a hard surface is 25.____

    A. rolled steel
    B. forged steel
    C. wrought iron
    D. cast iron

26. When using a portable electric drill having a 3-conductor cord, it is IMPORTANT from a safety point of view that 26.____

    A. the drill is run at fairly slow speeds
    B. high-speed drill bits should be used

C. the power outlet has a ground connection
D. the drill is run on 3-phase current

27. The MOST efficient way of laying out a 25-foot long, straight line on a concrete floor is to

    A. use a carpenter's pencil and a steel tape
    B. lay out a cord and mark the line with a crayon
    C. use chalk and a 6-foot ruler
    D. snap it on with a chalked mason's line

28. The MAIN advantage of using pipes instead of timber for temporary scaffolding is that pipe scaffolding

    A. requires no painting
    B. is easier to assemble and disassemble
    C. requires no bracing
    D. looks better

29. In order to avoid damage to an air compressor, the air coming into it is USUALLY

    A. cooled   B. metered   C. filtered   D. heated

30. If a gear having 24 teeth is revolving at 150 r.p.m., then the speed of an 8-tooth pinion driving the gear is _____ r.p.m.

    A. 50   B. 300   C. 450   D. 1200

31. To preserve wood from rotting, it is BEST to use

    A. aluminum paint   B. red lead
    C. rosin   D. creosote

32. On a two-stage air compressor, the intercooler is connected to the compressor unit

    A. *between* the two stages
    B. *after* the second stage
    C. *before* the first stage
    D. *between* the receiver and the outlet

33. Teflon is COMMONLY used as a(n)

    A. protective coating on ceramic plumbing fixtures
    B. sealer on threaded pipe joints
    C. additive to engine lubricating oil
    D. penetrating oil for rusting parts

34. A marline spike is GENERALLY used to

    A. splice manila rope
    B. fasten a heavy metal part to a wood panel wall
    C. shift large crates
    D. anchor wooden items to a concrete wall

35. A screw having double threads is one that

    A. should never be used for fastening sheet metal parts
    B. has two parallel threads running in the same direction
    C. has a right hand and a left hand thread
    D. can be used with a mating single-threaded nut

36. If the diameter of a circular piece of sheet metal is 1 1/2 feet, the area, in square inches, is MOST NEARLY

    A. 1.77 B. 2.36 C. 254 D. 324

37. When removing a cartridge-type fuse from the fuse clips in a circuit, it is important to use a fuse-puller PRIMARILY to avoid

    A. blowing the fuse
    B. damaging the fuse
    C. arcing
    D. personal injury

38. The MOST probable cause for the breaking of a drill bit while drilling into a steel plate is

    A. excessive drill pressure
    B. a hard spot in the steel
    C. a drill speed which is too low
    D. too much cutting-oil lubricant

39. In assembling structural steel, a drift pin is used to

    A. line up holes
    B. punch holes
    C. temporarily hold welded parts
    D. knock out structural bolts

40. The TIGHTEST fit for a mating shaft and hole is a _____ fit.

    A. running B. sliding C. working D. force

KEY (CORRECT ANSWERS)

1.	C	11.	B	21.	C	31.	D
2.	A	12.	D	22.	A	32.	A
3.	C	13.	C	23.	B	33.	B
4.	D	14.	A	24.	D	34.	A
5.	A	15.	D	25.	D	35.	B
6.	D	16.	D	26.	C	36.	C
7.	A	17.	B	27.	D	37.	D
8.	A	18.	B	28.	B	38.	A
9.	B	19.	B	29.	C	39.	A
10.	C	20.	A	30.	C	40.	D

TEST 2

DIRECTIONS: Each question or incomplete statement is followed by several suggested answers or completions. Select the one that BEST answers the question or completes the statement. *PRINT THE LETTER OF THE CORRECT ANSWER IN THE SPACE AT THE RIGHT.*

1. The crankshaft in a gasoline engine is PRIMARILY used to

    A. change reciprocating motion to rotary motion
    B. operate the valve lifters
    C. supply power to each cylinder
    D. function as a flywheel

2. Copper tubing is GENERALLY used in an annealed condition because annealing

    A. gives the copper tubing a protective finish
    B. makes the copper tubing harder
    C. provides a smoother surface on the inner and outer walls
    D. makes the copper tubing more ductile

3. Of the following, the MOST important advantage of a ratchet wrench as compared to an open-end wrench is that the ratchet wrench

    A. is adjustable
    B. cannot strip the threads of a nut
    C. can be used in a limited space
    D. measures the force applied

4. To provide a close-fitting hole for a taper pin, it is BEST to first drill the hole and then to use the appropriate

    A. hone   B. reamer
    C. boring tool   D. counterboring tool

5. If a part that is being checked for size fits loosely into a *NO-GO* gauge, it means that the

    A. part is the proper size
    B. part must be made smaller
    C. part is the wrong size
    D. gauge should be tightened

6. A hacksaw blade with 32 teeth per inch is BEST for cutting

    A. materials less than 1/8-inch thick
    B. a 3-inch diameter brass bar
    C. 1" thick copper plates
    D. a 3-inch diameter steel bar

7. The BEST method to follow in order to prevent a drill from wandering upon starting to drill a hole in a steel plate is to

    A. use a high-speed drill
    B. first use a center-punch

C. use a drill with even cutting angles
D. exert heavy pressure when drilling

8. When grinding a tool, it is GOOD practice to keep moving the tool across the face of the grinding wheel in order to

   A. prevent the tool from becoming too hot
   B. avoid sparks
   C. maintain a uniform grinding speed
   D. prevent grooving the wheel

9. A material that is COMMONLY used as a lining for bearings in order to reduce friction is

   A. magnesium   B. cast iron
   C. babbitt   D. carborundum

10. In a motor having sleeve bearings, bearing wear can be checked by measuring the air-gap clearance between the armature and the

    A. pole pieces   B. commutator
    C. bearing   D. brushes

11. If the scale on a shop drawing is 1/4 inch to the foot, then the length of a part which measures 2 3/8 inches long on the drawing is ACTUALLY _____ feet.

    A. 9 1/2   B. 8 1/2   C. 7 1/4   D. 4 1/4

12. When welding cast iron with an oxy-acetylene torch, the BEST weld is obtained when the cast iron is

    A. not preheated
    B. preheated slowly
    C. chilled quickly after welding
    D. chilled slowly after welding

13. A substance which can do the MOST damage to wire rope is

    A. acid   B. grease   C. gasoline   D. oil

14. When comparing the same nominal size of extra strong iron pipe with standard iron pipe, the extra strong iron pipe has _____ diameter _____ diameter.

    A. the same inside; but a larger outside
    B. the same outside; but a smaller inside
    C. a larger outside; and a smaller inside
    D. a larger inside; and a larger outside

15. A *Lally* column which is used in building construction consists of

    A. a large diameter pipe fitted with a base plate at each end
    B. channels tied with lattice bars
    C. unequal sections of round pipe
    D. angles and plates

16. On a 10-24 x 7/8" screw, the number 10 indicates that the size of the outside diameter is MOST NEARLY

    A. 0.187"   B. 10/64"   C. 10/32"   D. 0.10"

17. The liquid solution in an electrical storage battery MOST commonly is

    A. alkali
    B. acid
    C. pure distilled water
    D. copper sulphate

18. Manifolds on an internal combustion engine are used

    A. to mount the engine to the frame
    B. for cooling the engine
    C. in the carburetor
    D. to conduct gases into and out of the engine

19. For winter servicing of a gasoline engine, it is BEST to use an oil that

    A. has a low SAE number
    B. has a high SAE number
    C. has a very heavy consistency
    D. contains few additive detergents

20. To remove a slotted collar having internal threads from a shaft, the BEST of the following wrenches to use is a(n) _____ wrench.

    A. Allen   B. Stillson   C. socket   D. spanner

21. When using a heavy jack placed on the ground to raise a heavy load, it is important to place a sturdy, flat board under the jack PRIMARILY in order to

    A. facilitate placing the jack under the load
    B. reduce the jacking effort
    C. prevent the jack from slipping out from under the load
    D. decrease the jacking height

22. The pulley wheels of a block and tackle are COMMONLY called

    A. stocks   B. swivels   C. sheaves   D. guides

23. If the diameter of a machined part must be 1.035 ± 0.003", then it is ACCEPTABLE if it measures

    A. 1.031"   B. 1.032"   C. 1.039"   D. 1.335"

24. The type of threads for ordinary screws are USUALLY the _____ type.

    A. square   B. buttress   C. V   D. Acme

25. Lead is NORMALLY used in caulking _____ pipe.

    A. copper
    B. brass
    C. steel
    D. cast iron

26. Of the following materials, the one which is COMMONLY used as a lubricant is

    A. powdered iron oxide   B. powdered graphite
    C. casein   D. rosin flux

27. On grinders, the tool rest is generally 1/8-inch from the face of the wheel. When dressing small parts on grinders, greater clearance is usually undesirable, because too much clearance may cause

    A. the work piece to jam and break the wheel
    B. material from the work piece to be ground off too rapidly
    C. the cutting action of the grinder to be hidden from view
    D. scoring of the wheel

28. The BEST way to determine whether the locknuts on terminals in an electrical terminal box have become loose is to

    A. use an electric tester
    B. try to tighten the nuts with an appropriate wrench
    C. tap the nuts with an insulated handle
    D. try to loosen the nuts with a pair of pliers

29. It is necessary to pour a new concrete floor for a shop. If the dimensions of the concrete slab for the floor are to be 27' x 18' x 6", then the number of cubic yards of concrete that must be poured is

    A. 9   B. 16   C. 54   D. 243

30. The jaws of a vise move 1/4" for each complete turn of the handle. The number of complete turns necessary to open the jaws 2 3/4" is

    A. 9   B. 10   C. 11   D. 12

31. The sum of 5'6", 7'3", 9' 3 1/2", and 3' 7 1/4" is

    A. 19' 8 1/2"   B. 22' 1/2"   C. 25' 7 3/4"   D. 28' 8 3/4"

32. Of the following statements describing the use of carbon dioxide type fire extinguishers, the one which is TRUE is that they

    A. may be used on grease fires
    B. should not be used to extinguish electrical fires
    C. can not be used on most types of fires
    D. are ideal for use in poorly ventilated areas

33. The PRIMARY reason for a twist drill *splitting up the center* is that the

    A. cutting edges were ground at different angles
    B. lips were ground at different lengths
    C. lip clearance angle was too great
    D. lip clearance angle was insufficient

34. The PROPER file a machinist should use for finishing ordinary flat surfaces is the _____ file.

    A. Pillar   B. Warding
    C. Hooktooth   D. Hand

35. An all hard saw blade should be used in a hacksaw frame when sawing

    A. tool steel
    B. channel iron
    C. aluminum
    D. thin wall copper tubing

36. The surface gage is generally NOT used for

    A. laying out
    B. leveling and lining up work
    C. checking angles and tapers
    D. locating centers on rough work

Questions 37-40.

DIRECTIONS: The sketch shown below refers to a piping arrangement for connecting a new space heater. Questions 37 through 40 are based on it.

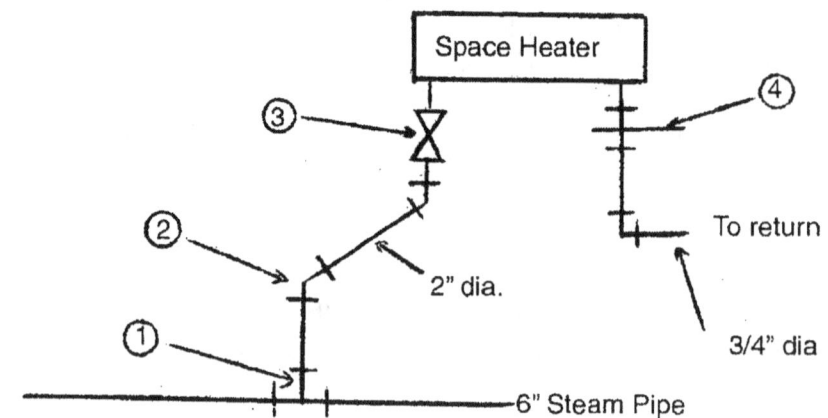

37. Pipe fitting 1 is a

    A. bull tee
    B. sanitary tee
    C. reducing tee
    D. cross

38. Pipe fitting 2 is a

    A. branch tee
    B. Y fitting
    C. right elbow
    D. 45 degree elbow

39. Pipe fitting 3 is a

    A. coupling
    B. flange
    C. valve
    D. steam trap

40. Pipe fitting 4 is a

    A. union   B. valve   C. tee   D. reducer

KEY (CORRECT ANSWERS)

1.	A	11.	A	21.	C	31.	C
2.	D	12.	B	22.	C	32.	A
3.	C	13.	A	23.	B	33.	D
4.	B	14.	B	24.	C	34.	D
5.	C	15.	A	25.	D	35.	A
6.	A	16.	A	26.	B	36.	C
7.	B	17.	B	27.	A	37.	C
8.	D	18.	D	28.	B	38.	D
9.	C	19.	A	29.	A	39.	C
10.	A	20.	D	30.	C	40.	A

EXAMINATION SECTION
TEST 1

DIRECTIONS: Each question or incomplete statement is followed by several suggested answers or completions. Select the one that BEST answers the question or completes the statement. *PRINT THE LETTER OF THE CORRECT ANSWER IN THE SPACE AT THE RIGHT.*

1. Asbestos was used as a covering on electrical wires to provide protection from   1._____

    A. high voltage
    B. high temperature
    C. water damage
    D. electrolysis

2. The rating term *240 volts, 10 H.P.* would be PROPERLY used to describe a   2._____

    A. transformer
    B. storage battery
    C. motor
    D. rectifier

3. Rigid steel conduit used for the protection of electrical wiring is GENERALLY either galvanized or enameled both inside and out in order to   3._____

    A. prevent damage to the wire insulation
    B. make threading of the conduit easier
    C. prevent corrosion of the conduit
    D. make the conduit easier to handle

4. BX is COMMONLY used to indicate   4._____

    A. rigid conduit without wires
    B. flexible conduit without wires
    C. insulated wires covered with flexible steel armor
    D. insulated wires covered with a non-metallic covering

5. If a test lamp does not light when placed in series with a fuse and an appropriate battery, it is a GOOD indication that the fuse   5._____

    A. is open-circuited
    B. is short-circuited
    C. is in operating condition
    D. has zero resistance

6. Of the following, the SIMPLEST wood joint to make is a   6._____

    A. half lap joint
    B. mortise and tenon
    C. butt joint
    D. multiple dovetail

7. To accurately cut a number of lengths of wood at an angle of 45 degrees, it would be BEST to use a   7._____

    A. protractor
    B. mitre-box
    C. triangle
    D. square

8. The soffit of a beam is the   8._____

    A. span   B. side   C. bottom   D. top

9. A nail set is a tool used for
   A. straightening bent nails
   B. cutting nails to specified size
   C. sinking a nail head in wood
   D. measuring nail size

10. It is UNLAWFUL to
    A. use wooden lath
    B. have ceiling lath run in one direction only
    C. break joints when using wood lath
    D. run wood lath through from room to room

11. A concrete mix for a construction job requires a certain ratio of cement, water, sand, and small stones.
    The MOST serious error in mixing would be to use 20% too much
    A. sand
    B. water
    C. small stones
    D. mixing time

12. Impurities in a mortar which may seriously affect its strength are MOST likely to enter the mortar with the
    A. mixing water
    B. sand
    C. lime
    D. gypsum

13. One ADVANTAGE of using plywood instead of boards for concrete forms is that plywood
    A. needs no bracing
    B. does not split easily
    C. sticks less to concrete
    D. insulates concrete against freezing

14. Concrete will crack MOST easily when it is subject to
    A. compression
    B. bearing
    C. bonding
    D. tension

15. Where a smooth dense finish is desired for a concrete surface, it will BEST be produced by using a
    A. wood float
    B. level
    C. steel trowel
    D. vibrator

16. Sewer gas is prevented from backing up through a fixture by a
    A. water trap
    B. vent pipe
    C. check valve
    D. float valve

17. Packing is used in an adjustable water valve MAINLY to
    A. make it air-tight
    B. prevent mechanical wear
    C. regulate the water pressure
    D. make it water-tight

18. Good practice requires that the end of a piece of water pipe be reamed to remove the inside burr after it has been cut to length.
The PURPOSE of the reaming is to

    A. finish the pipe accurately to length
    B. make the threading easier
    C. avoid cutting of the workers' hands
    D. allow free passage for the flow of water

19. The MAIN reason for pitching a steam pipe in a heating system is to

    A. prevent accumulation of condensed steam
    B. present a smaller radiating surface
    C. facilitate repairs
    D. reduce friction in the pipe

20. When fitting pipe together, poor alignment of pipe and fittings would MOST likely result in

    A. leaky joints
    B. cracking of the pipe on expansion
    C. formation of hot spots
    D. cracking of the pipe on contraction

21. Roofing nails are GENERALLY

    A. brass plated
    B. galvanized
    C. cement coated
    D. nickel plated

22. Specifications for a roofing job call for 3 *lbs. sheet lead*. This means that each sheet SHOULD weigh 3 lbs. per

    A. square inch
    B. square foot
    C. square yard
    D. sheet

23. The MAIN reason for using flashing at the intersection of different roof planes is to

    A. increase the durability of the shingles
    B. simplify the installation of the shingles
    C. waterproof the roof
    D. improve the appearance of the roof

24. Of the following roofing materials, the one that is MOST frequently used in *built-up* roofs is

    A. asbestos shingles
    B. three-ply felt
    C. sheet copper
    D. wood sheathing

25. As used in roofing, *a square* refers to

    A. a tool for lining up the roofing with the eaves of the house
    B. one hundred square feet of roofing
    C. one hundred shingles of roofing
    D. one hundred pounds of roofing

26. In the process of replacing a pane of window glass, the old putty should be scraped off the window sash and the wood surfaces then primed with

   A. resin oil
   B. shellac
   C. linseed oil
   D. enamel

27. The LARGEST available size of glazier's points is number

   A. 3   B. 1   C. 0   D. 000

28. The purpose of priming wood window sash before applying putty and glass is to prevent the

   A. putty from absorbing moisture from the wood
   B. putty from staining the wood
   C. wood from absorbing the oils from the putty
   D. natural wood resins from making the putty brittle

29. When hard, dry putty must be removed from a wood window frame in order to put in a new pane of glass, the BEST tool with which to do this job is a

   A. screwdriver
   B. putty knife
   C. wide wood chisel
   D. pocket knife

30. Before repainting a wood surface on which the old paint film has developed some wrinkling, the MOST appropriate treatment for the wood surface is a

   A. thorough scraping
   B. light shellacking
   C. wash-down with dilute muriatic acid
   D. rubbing down of the wrinkles with fairly coarse sand-paper

31. A paint that is characterized by its ability to dry to an especially smooth, hard, glossy or semi-glossy finish is called a(n)

   A. primer   B. sealer   C. glaze   D. enamel

32. The BEST thinner for varnish is

   A. gasoline
   B. turpentine
   C. kerosene
   D. water

33. To get a good paint job on a new plaster wall, one should make certain that the

   A. wall is thoroughly dry before painting
   B. base coat is much darker than the finishing coat
   C. wall has been roughened enough to make the paint stick
   D. plaster has not completely set

34. In a three-coat plaster job, the brown coat is applied

   A. before the scratch coat has set
   B. immediately after the scratch coat
   C. after the scratch coat has set and partially dried
   D. after the scratch coat has thoroughly dried out

35. Plaster which has sand as an aggregate, when compared with plaster which has a light-weight aggregate, is

   A. a better sound absorber
   B. a better insulator
   C. less likely to crack under a sharp blow
   D. cheaper

36. One form of metal lath comes in sheets 27" x 96".
    The number of sheets required to cover 20 square yards without overlap is

    A. 9   B. 10   C. 11   D. 12

37. When nailing gypsum board lath to studs or furring strips, the nailing should be started_____ of the board.

    A. along the top   B. along the bottom
    C. at the center   D. at one end

38. A wooden mortar box for slaking lime is lined with sheet iron.
    Of the following, the GREATEST advantage of the lining is that

    A. a better grade putty is produced
    B. the box is easier to clean
    C. it makes the box water-tight
    D. it prevents burning of the wood

39. The Building Code requires that water used in plastering MUST

    A. be perfectly clear in color
    B. not have any rust in it
    C. be fit for drinking
    D. not be fluoridated

40. In order to prevent thin sheet metal from buckling when riveting it to an angle iron, the BEST procedure is to

    A. start riveting at one end of the sheet and work toward the other end
    B. start riveting at both ends of the sheet and work in toward the center
    C. install alternate rivets working in one direction, and then fill in the remaining rivets working in the other direction
    D. start riveting in the center of the joint, working out in both directions

KEY (CORRECT ANSWERS)

1. B	11. B	21. B	31. D
2. C	12. B	22. B	32. B
3. C	13. B	23. C	33. A
4. C	14. D	24. B	34. C
5. A	15. C	25. B	35. D
6. C	16. A	26. C	36. B
7. B	17. D	27. C	37. C
8. C	18. D	28. C	38. B
9. C	19. A	29. C	39. C
10. D	20. A	30. D	40. D

TEST 2

DIRECTIONS: Each question or incomplete statement is followed by several suggested answers or completions. Select the one that BEST answers the question or completes the statement. *PRINT THE LETTER OF THE CORRECT ANSWER IN THE SPACE AT THE RIGHT.*

1. A drill bit measures .625 inches. 1.____
   The FRACTIONAL EQUIVALENT, in inches, is

   A. 9/16   B. 5/8   C. 11/16   D. 3/4

2. The number of cubic yards of sand required to fill a bin measuring 12 feet by 6 feet by 4 feet is MOST NEARLY 2.____

   A. 8   B. 11   C. 48   D. 96

3. Assume that you are assigned to put down floor tiles in a room measuring 8 feet by 10 feet. Individual tiles measure 9 inches by 9 inches. 3.____
   The total number of floor tiles required to cover the entire floor is MOST NEARLY

   A. 107   B. 121   C. 144   D. 160

4. Lumber is usually sold by the board foot, and a board foot is defined as a board one foot square and one inch thick. 4.____
   If the price of one board foot of lumber is 18 cents and you need 20 feet of lumber 6 inches wide and 1 inch thick, the cost of the 20 feet of the lumber is

   A. $1.80   B. $2.40   C. $3.60   D. $4.80

5. For a certain plumbing repair job, you need three lengths of pipe, 12 1/4 inches, 6 1/2 inches, and 8 5/8 inches. 5.____
   If you cut these three lengths from the same piece of pipe, which is 36 inches long, and each cut consumes 1/8 inch of pipe, the length of pipe REMAINING after you have cut out your three pieces should be _____ inches.

   A. 7 1/4   B. 7 7/8   C. 8 1/4   D. 8 7/8

6. Glazier points are small pieces of galvanized metal often having the shape of a(n) 6.____

   A. circle   B. ellipse   C. square   D. triangle

7. Putty that is too stiff is made workable by adding 7.____

   A. gasoline   B. linseed oil
   C. water   D. lacquer thinner

8. Soap is applied to wood screws before they are used in order to 8.____

   A. prevent rust
   B. make a tight fit
   C. make insertion easier
   D. prevent screws from loosening after insertion

9. A method sometimes used to prevent a pipe from buckling during a bending operation is to 9.____

A. bend the pipe very quickly
B. keep the seam of the pipe on the outside of the bend
C. nick the pipe at the center of the bend
D. pack the inside of the pipe with sand

10. Rubber gaskets are frequently placed between the faces of the flanges when making up a flanged joint in a pipe line in order to

A. prevent corrosion of the machined faces
B. permit full tightening of the flange bolts without danger of thread stripping
C. eliminate the necessity for accurate alignment of the pipe
D. make a tight joint

11. A parapet is the

A. stepping out of successive courses of brickwork
B. continuation of a wall above the roof line
C. wall enclosing stairs that lead to the roof
D. portion of an exterior wall below a window

12. The process of removing the insulation from a wire is called

A. braiding   B. skinning   C. sweating   D. tinning

13. The process of making fresh concrete watertight, durable, and strong after it has been poured is called

A. air-entraining   B. finishing
C. curing   D. accelerating

14. A mixture of cement, sand, and water is called

A. hydrated lime   B. plain concrete
C. hydrated cement   D. mortar

15. The *grip* applied to a pipe with gas pliers is increased by using pliers with

A. longer handles   B. larger jaws
C. thicker handles   D. larger teeth

16. Those materials which are added to a paint vehicle to regulate its consistency and thus increase its spreading power and facilitate its application are called

A. driers   B. thinners
C. extenders   D. oxidents

17. The fitting which usually is easiest to disconnect FIRST when disassembling a piping run is a(n)

A. cross   B. union
C. return bend   D. elbow

18. For convenience in case of future repairs to a long pipe line, it is DESIRABLE to fit the pipe together with several

A. street ells   B. elbows
C. return bends   D. unions

19. If four pipes are to be connected into each other at a common point, it would be NECESSARY to use a(n)

   A. tee fitting
   B. street ell
   C. cross
   D. offset

20. The BEST of the following tools to use for cutting off a piece of single conductor #6 rubber insulated lead covered cable is a

   A. pair of electrician's pliers
   B. hacksaw
   C. hammer and cold chisel
   D. lead knife

21. One ADVANTAGE of rubber insulation is that it

   A. does not deteriorate with age
   B. is able to withstand high temperature
   C. does not absorb much moisture
   D. is not damaged by oil

22. The SIMPLEST device for interrupting an overloaded electrical circuit is a

   A. fuse
   B. relay
   C. capacitor
   D. choke-coil

23. Reinforced concrete USUALLY means concrete that has been strengthened by use of

   A. additional cement
   B. steel bars
   C. extra heavy gravel
   D. high strength cement

24. A VERTICAL wood member in the wall of a wood frame house is known as a

   A. stringer
   B. ridge member
   C. stud
   D. header

25. A riser is GENERALLY a pipe run which is

   A. horizontal
   B. curved
   C. vertical
   D. at a 45-degree angle

26. A standard pipe thread DIFFERS from a standard screw thread in that the pipe thread

   A. is tapered
   B. is deeper
   C. requires no lubrication when cutting
   D. has the same pitch for any diameter of pipe

27. The material which is LEAST likely to be found in use as the outer covering of rubber insulated wires or cables is

   A. cotton
   B. varnished cambric
   C. lead
   D. neoprene

28. In measuring to determine the size of a standard insulated conductor, the PROPER place to use the wire gauge is on

A. the insulation
B. the outer covering
C. the stranded conductor
D. one strand of the conductor

29. Rubber insulation on an electrical conductor would MOST quickly be damaged by continuous contact with

    A. acid   B. water   C. oil   D. alkali

30. If a fuse clip becomes hot under normal circuit load, the MOST probable cause is that the

    A. clip makes poor contact with the fuse ferrule
    B. circuit wires are too small
    C. current rating of the fuse is too high
    D. voltage rating of the fuse is too low

31. If the input to a 10 to 1 step-down transformer is 15 amperes at 2400 volts, the secondary output would be NEAREST to _____ amperes at _____ volts.

    A. 1.5; 24,000
    B. 150; 240
    C. 1.5; 240
    D. 150; 24,000

32. The resistance of a copper wire to the flow of electricity _____ as the_____ of the wire _____.

    A. increases; diameter; increases
    B. decreases; diameter; decreases
    C. decreases; length; increases
    D. increases; length; increases

33. Where galvanized steel conduit is used, the PRIMARY purpose of the galvanizing is to

    A. increase mechanical strength
    B. retard rusting
    C. provide a good surface for painting
    D. provide good electrical contact for grounding

34. The lamps used for station and tunnel lighting in the subways are generally operated at slightly less than their rated voltage.
    The LOGICAL reason for this is to

    A. prevent overloading of circuits
    B. increase the life of the lamps
    C. decrease glare
    D. obtain a more even distribution of light

35. The CORRECT method of measuring the power taken by an a.c. electric motor is to use a

    A. wattmeter
    B. voltmeter and an ammeter
    C. power factor meter
    D. tachometer

36. Wood ladders should NOT be painted because the paint

   A. may deteriorate the wood
   B. makes the ladders slippery
   C. is inflammable
   D. may cover cracks or defects

37. Goggles would be LEAST necessary when

   A. recharging soda-acid fire extinguishers
   B. chipping stone
   C. putting electrolyte into an Edison battery
   D. scraping rubber insulation from a wire

38. The number and type of precautions to be taken on a job generally depend LEAST on the

   A. nature of the job
   B. length of time the job is expected to last
   C. kind of tools and materials being used
   D. location of the work

39. When training workers in the use of tools and equipment, safety precautions related to their use should be FIRST mentioned

   A. in the introductory training session before the workers begin to use the equipment or tools
   B. during training sessions when workers practice operating the tools or equipment
   C. after the workers are qualified to use the equipment in their daily tasks
   D. when an agency safety bulletin related to the tools and equipment is received

40. Many portable electric power tools, such as electric drills, have a third conductor in the power lead which is used to connect the case of the tool to a grounded part of the electric outlet.
    The reason for this extra conductor is to

   A. have a spare wire in case one power wire should break
   B. strengthen the power lead so it cannot easily be damaged
   C. prevent the user of the tool from being shocked
   D. enable the tool to be used for long periods of time without overheating

KEY (CORRECT ANSWERS)

1.	B	11.	B	21.	C	31.	B
2.	B	12.	B	22.	A	32.	D
3.	C	13.	C	23.	B	33.	B
4.	A	14.	D	24.	C	34.	B
5.	C	15.	A	25.	C	35.	A
6.	D	16.	B	26.	A	36.	D
7.	B	17.	B	27.	B	37.	D
8.	C	18.	D	28.	D	38.	B
9.	D	19.	C	29.	C	39.	A
10.	D	20.	B	30.	A	40.	C

———

ARITHMETICAL REASONING
EXAMINATION SECTION
TEST 1

DIRECTIONS: Each question or incomplete statement is followed by several suggested answers or completions. Select the one that BEST answers the question or completes the statement. *PRINT THE LETTER OF THE CORRECT ANSWER IN THE SPACE AT THE RIGHT.*

1. A supplier quotes a list price of $172.00 less 15 and 10 percent for twelve tools. The actual cost for these twelve tools is MOST NEARLY

   A. $146   B. $132   C. $129   D. $112

2. If the diameter of a circular piece of sheet metal is 1 1/2 feet, the area, in square inches, is MOST NEARLY

   A. 1.77   B. 2.36   C. 254   D. 324

3. The sum of 5'6", 7'3", 9'3 1/2", and 3'7 1/4" is

   A. 19'8 1/2"   B. 22' 1/2"   C. 25'7 3/4"   D. 28'8 3/4"

4. If the floor area of one shop is 15' by 21'3" and the size of an adjacent shop is 18' by 30'6", then the TOTAL floor area of these two shops is _____ square feet.

   A. 1127.75   B. 867.75   C. 549.0   D. 318.75

5. The fraction which is equal to 0.875 is

   A. 7/16   B. 5/8   C. 3/4   D. 7/8

6. The sum of 1/2, 2 1/32, 4 3/16, and 1 7/8 is MOST NEARLY

   A. 9.593   B. 9.625   C. 9.687   D. 10.593

7. If the base of a right triangle is 9" and the altitude is 12", the length of the third side will be

   A. 13"   B. 14"   C. 15"   D. 16"

8. If a steel bar 1" in diameter and 12' long weighs 32 lbs., then the weight of a piece of this bar 5'9" long is MOST NEARLY _____ lbs.

   A. 15.33   B. 15.26   C. 16.33   D. 15.06

9. The diameter of a circle whose circumference is 12" is MOST NEARLY

   A. 3.82"   B. 3.72"   C. 3.62"   D. 3.52"

10. A dimension of 39/64 inches converted to decimals is MOST NEARLY

    A. .600"   B. .609"   C. .607"   D. .611"

11. A farm worker was paid a weekly wage of $415.20 for a 44-hour work week. As a result of a new labor contract, he is paid $431.40 a week for a 40-hour work week with time and one-half pay for time worked in excess of 40 hours in any work week.
    If he continues to work 44 hours weekly under the new contract, the amount by which his average hourly rate for a 44-hour work week under the new contract exceeds the hourly rate previously paid him lies between _____ and _____, inclusive.

    A. 80¢; $1.00
    B. $1.00; $1.20
    C. $1.25; $1.45
    D. $1.50; $1.70

12. The sum of 4 feet 3 1/4 inches, 7 feet 2 1/2 inches, and 11 feet 1/4 inch is _____ feet _____ inches.

    A. 21; 6 1/4   B. 22; 6   C. 23; 5   D. 24; 5 3/4

13. The number 0.038 is read as

    A. 38 tenths
    B. 38 hundredths
    C. 38 thousandths
    D. 38 ten-thousandths

14. Assume that an employee is paid at the rate of $10.86 per hour with time and a half for overtime past 40 hours in a week.
    If he works 43 hours in a week, his gross weekly pay is

    A. $434.40   B. $438.40   C. $459.18   D. $483.27

15. The sum of the following dimensions: 3'2 1/4", 8 7/8", 2'6 3/8", 2'9 3/4", and 1'0" is

    A. 16'7 1/4"   B. 10'7 1/4"   C. 10'3 1/4"   D. 9'3 1/4"

16. Two gears are meshed together and have a gear ratio of 6 to 1.
    If the small gear rotates 120 revolutions per minute, the large gear rotates at

    A. 20   B. 40   C. 60   D. 720

17. The vacuum side of a compound gage reads 14 inches of vacuum. The barometer reading is 29.76 inches of mercury. The equivalent absolute pressure of the compound gage reading, in inches of mercury, is MOST likely

    A. 15.06   B. 15.76   C. 43.06   D. 43.76

18. The fraction 5/8 expressed as a decimal is

    A. 0.125   B. 0.412   C. 0.625   D. 0.875

19. If 300 feet of a certain size pipe weighs 450 pounds, the number of pounds that 100 feet will weigh is

    A. 1,350   B. 150   C. 300   D. 250

20. As an oiler, you work for a facility that has automobiles that use, on the average, 600 quarts of one grade of lubricating oil every month.
    The number of one-gallon cans of the above oil that should be ordered each month to meet this requirement is

    A. 100   B. 125   C. 140   D. 150

21. The inside dimensions of a rectangular oil gravity tank are: height 15", width 9", length 10".
The amount of oil in the tank, in gallons, (231 cu.in. = 1 gallon), when the oil level is 9" high, is MOST NEARLY

    A. 2.3 B. 3.5 C. 5.2 D. 5.8

22. If 30 gallons of oil cost $76.80, 45 gallons of oil at the same rate will cost

    A. $91.20 B. $115.20 C. $123.20 D. $131.20

23. If an oiler earns $18,000 in the first six months of a year and receives a 10% raise in salary for the next six months of the same year, his TOTAL earnings for the year will be

    A. $36,000 B. $37,500 C. $37,800 D. $39,600

24. If the cost of lubricating oil increases 15%, then a gallon of oil which used to cost $10.00 will now cost MOST NEARLY

    A. $10.50 B. $11.00 C. $11.50 D. $12.00

25. The sum of 7/8", 3/4", 1/2", and 3/8" is

    A. 2 1/8" B. 2 1/4" C. 2 3/8" D. 2 1/2"

KEY (CORRECT ANSWERS)

1. B		11. A	
2. C		12. B	
3. C		13. C	
4. B		14. D	
5. D		15. C	
6. A		16. A	
7. C		17. B	
8. A		18. C	
9. A		19. B	
10. B		20. D	

21. B
22. B
23. C
24. C
25. D

SOLUTIONS TO PROBLEMS

1. Actual cost = ($172)(.85)(.90) = $131.58 ≈ $132

2. Radius = .75', then area = (3.14)(.75)^2 ≈ 1.77 sq.ft.
   Since 1 sq.ft. = 144 sq.in., the area ≈ 254 sq.in.

3. 5'6" + 7'3" + 9'3 1/2" + 3'7 1/4" = 24'19 3/4" = 25'7 3/4"

4. Total area = (15)(21.25) + (18)(30.5) = 867.75 sq.ft.

5. .875 = 875/1000 = 7/8

6. 1 1/2 + 2 1/32 + 4 3/16 + 1 7/8 = 8 51/32 = 9 19/32 = 9.593

7. Third side = $\sqrt{9^2 + 12^2} = \sqrt{225} = 15$"

8. Let x = weight. Then, 12/32 = 5.75/x. Solving, x ≈ 15.33 lbs.

9. 12" = (3.14)(diameter), so diameter ≈ 3.82"

10. $\frac{39}{64}$" = .609375" ≈ .609"

11. Under his new contract, the weekly wage for 44 hours can be found by first determining his hourly rate for the first 40 hours = $431.40 ÷ 40 ≈ $10.80. Now, his time and one-half pay will = ($10.80)(1.5) = $16.20. His weekly wage for the new contract = $431.40 + (4)($16.20) = $496.20. His new hourly rate for 44 hours = $496.20 ÷ 44 ≈ $10.34. Under the old contract, his hourly rate for 44 hours was $415.20 ÷ 44 = $9.44. His hourly rate increase = $10.34 - $9.44 = $0.90. (Answer key: between $0.80 and $1.00)

12. 4'3 1/4" + 7'2 1/2" + 11' 1/4" = 22'6"

13. .038 = 38 thousandths

14. ($10.86)(40) + ($16.29)(3) = $483.27

15. 3'2 1/4" + 8 7/8" + 2'6 3/8" + 2'9 3/4" + 1'0" = 8'25 18/8" = 10'3 1/4"

16. The gear ratio is inversely proportional to the gear size. Let x = large gear's rpm. Then, 6/1 = 120/x. Solving, x = 20

17. Subtract 14 from 29.76

18. 5/8 = .625

19. Let x = number of pounds. Then, 300/450 = 100/x. Solving, x = 150

20. 600 quarts = 150 gallons, since 4 quarts = 1 gallon

21. (9")(9")(10") = 810 cu.in. Then, 810 ÷ 231 ≈ 3.5

22. Let x = unknown cost. Then, 30/$76.80 = 45/x. Solving, x = $115.20

23. $18,000 + ($18,000)(1.10) = $37,800

24. ($10.00)(1.15) = $11.50

25. 7/8" + 3/4" + 1/2" + 3/8" = 20/8" = 2 1/2"

TEST 2

DIRECTIONS: Each question or incomplete statement is followed by several suggested answers or completions. Select the one that BEST answers the question or completes the statement. *PRINT THE LETTER OF THE CORRECT ANSWER IN THE SPACE AT THE RIGHT.*

1. A sheet metal plate has been cut in the form of a right triangle with sides of 5, 12, and 13 inches.
   The area of this plate, in square inches, is

   A. 30   B. 32 1/2   C. 60   D. 78

   1.____

2. If steel weighs 480 lbs. per cubic foot, the weight of an 18" x 18" x 2" steel base plate is _____ lbs.

   A. 180   B. 216   C. 427   D. 648

   2.____

3. By trial, it is found that by using 2 cubic feet of sand, a 5 cubic foot batch of concrete is produced.
   Using the same proportions, the amount of sand, in cubic feet, required to produce 2 cubic yards of concrete is MOST NEARLY

   A. 7   B. 22   C. 27   D. 45

   3.____

4. The total number of cubic yards of earth to be removed to make a trench 3'9" wide, 25'0" long, and 4'3" deep is MOST NEARLY

   A. 53.1   B. 35.4   C. 26.6   D. 14.8

   4.____

5. A large number of 2 x 4 studs, some 10'5" long and some 6'5 1/2" long, are required for a job.
   To minimize waste, it would be PREFERABLE to order lengths of _____ feet.

   A. 16   B. 17   C. 18   D. 19

   5.____

6. A 6" pipe is connected to a 4" pipe through a reducer. If 100 cubic feet of water is flowing through the 6" pipe per minute, the flow, in cubic feet, per minute through the 4" pipe is

   A. 225   B. 100   C. 66.6   D. 44.4

   6.____

7. If steel weighs 0.28 pounds per cubic inch, then the weight, in pounds, of a 2" square steel bar 120" long is MOST NEARLY

   A. 115   B. 125   C. 135   D. 155

   7.____

8. A three-inch diameter steel bar two feet long weighs MOST NEARLY (assume steel weighs 480 lbs./cu.ft.) _____ lbs.

   A. 48   B. 58   C. 68   D. 78

   8.____

9. The area of a circular plate will be reduced by 5% if a sector removed from it has an angle of _____ degrees.

   A. 18   B. 24   C. 32   D. 60

   9.____

10. If a 4 1/16 inch shaft wears six thousandths of an inch, the NEW diameter will be _____ inches.

   A. 4.0031   B. 4.0565   C. 4.0578   D. 4.0605

11. A set of mechanical plan drawings is drawn to a scale of 1/8" = 1 foot.
   If a length of pipe measures 15 7/16" on the drawing, the ACTUAL length of the pipe is _____ feet.

   A. 121.5   B. 122.5   C. 123.5   D. 124.5

12. An electrical drawing is drawn to a scale of 1/4" = 1'. If a length of conduit on the drawing measures 7 3/8", the actual length of the conduit, in feet, is

   A. 7.5   B. 15.5   C. 22.5   D. 29.5

13. Assume that you have assigned 6 mechanics to do a job that must be finished in 4 days. At the end of 3 days, your men have completed only two-thirds of the job. In order to complete the job on time and because the job is such that it cannot be speeded up, you should assign a MINIMUM of _____ extra men.

   A. 3   B. 4   C. 5   D. 6

14. Assume that a trench is 42" wide, 5' deep, and 100' long. If the unit price of excavating the trench is $105 per cubic yard, the cost of excavating the trench is MOST NEARLY

   A. $6,805   B. $15,330   C. $21,000   D. $63,000

15. If the scale on a shop drawing is 1/4 inch to the foot, then the length of a part which measures 2 3/8 inches long on the drawing is ACTUALLY _____ feet.

   A. 9 1/2   B. 8 1/2   C. 7 1/4   D. 4 1/4

16. It is necessary to pour a new concrete floor for a shop. If the dimensions of the concrete slab for the floor are to be 27' x 18' x 6", then the number of cubic yards of concrete that must be poured is

   A. 9   B. 16   C. 54   D. 243

17. The jaws of a vise move 1/4" for each complete turn of the handle.
   The number of complete turns necessary to open the jaws 2 3/4" is

   A. 9   B. 10   C. 11   D. 12

18. Assume that a jobbing shop is to submit a price for a contract involving 300 pieces of work. Assume that material costs 50 cents per piece, labor costs $7.50 an hour, and a lathe operator can complete 5 pieces in an hour.
   If overhead is 40% of material and labor costs and the profit is 10% of all costs, the submitted price for the entire job will be

   A. $630.24   B. $872.80   C. $900.00   D. $924.00

19. The following formula is used in connection with the three-wire method of measuring pitch diameters of screw threads: $G=\dfrac{0.57735}{N}$, where G = wire size and N = number of threads per inch.
According to this formula, the proper size of wire for a 1"-8NC thread is MOST NEARLY

   A. .0722"   B. .7217"   C. .0072"   D. .0074"

20. A millimeter is 1/25.4 of an inch and there are 10 millimeters to a centimeter. If a piece of stock measures 127 centimeters long, the length of the stock, in feet and inches, would be MOST NEARLY

   A. 2'1"   B. 4'2"   C. 8'4"   D. 41'8"

21. For a certain job, you will need 25 steel bars 1 inch in diameter and 4"6" long. If these bars weigh 3 pounds per foot of length, then the TOTAL weight for all 25 bars is _____ pounds.

   A. 13.5   B. 75.0   C. 112.5   D. 337.5

22. If steel weighs 0.30 pounds per cubic inch, then the weight of a 2 inch square steel bar 90 inches long is _____ pounds.

   A. 27   B. 54   C. 108   D. 360

23. A concrete wall is 36' long, 9' high, and 1 1/2' thick. The number of cubic yards of concrete that were needed to make this wall is

   A. 14   B. 18   C. 27   D. 36

24. If the scale on a shop drawing is 1/2 inch to the foot, then the length of a part which measures 4 1/4 inches long on the drawing has a length of APPROXIMATELY _____ feet.

   A. 2 1/8   B. 4 1/4   C. 8 1/2   D. 10 3/4

25. If the allowable load on a wooden scaffold is 60 pounds per square foot and the scaffold surface area is 3 feet by 12 feet, then the MAXIMUM total distributed load that is permitted on the scaffold is _____ pounds.

   A. 720   B. 1,800   C. 2,160   D. 2,400

KEY (CORRECT ANSWERS)

1. A
2. A
3. B
4. D
5. B

6. B
7. C
8. A
9. A
10. B

11. C
12. D
13. A
14. A
15. A

16. A
17. C
18. D
19. A
20. B

21. D
22. C
23. B
24. C
25. C

SOLUTIONS TO PROBLEMS

1. Area = (1/2)(base)(height) = (1/2)(5")(12") = 30 sq.in.

2. Volume = (18") (18") (2") = 648 cu.in. = 648/1720 cu.ft.
   Then, (480)(648/1720) = ≈ 180 lbs.

3. 2 cu.yds. = 54 cu.ft. Let x = required cubic feet of sand. Then, 2/5 = x/54. Solving, x = 21.6 (or about 22)

4. (3.75')(25')(4.25') = 398.4375 cu.ft. ≈ 14.8 cu.yds.

5. 10'5" + 6'5 1/2" = 16'10 1/2", so lengths of 17 feet are needed

6. The amount of water flowing through each pipe must be equal.

7. (2")(2")(120") = 480 cu. in. Then, (480)(.28) ≈ 135 lbs.

8. Volume = (π) (.125 ')^2 (2) ≈ .1 cu.ft. Then, (.1)(480) = 48 lbs.

9. (360°)(.05) - 18°

10. 4 1/16 - .006 = 4.0625 - .006 = 4.0565

11. 15 7/16" ÷ 1/8" = 247/16 . 8/1 = 123.5. Then, (123.5)(1 ft.) = 123.5 ft.

12. 7 3/8" ÷ 1/4" = 59/8 . 4/1 = 29.5 Then, (29.5)(1 ft.) = 29.5 ft.

13. (6)(4) = 24 man-days normally required. Since after 3 days only the equivalent of (2/3)(24) = 16 man-days of work has been 1 done, 8 man-days of work is still left. 16 ÷ 3 = 5 1/3, which means the crew is equivalent to only 5 1/3 men. To do the 8 man-days of work, it will require at least 8 - 5 1/3 = 2 2/3 = 3 additional men.

14. (3.5')(5')(100') = 1750 cu.ft. ≈ 64.8 cu.yds. Then, (64.8)($105) ≈ $6805

15. 2 3/8" ÷ 1/4" = 19/8 . 4/1 = 9 1/2 Then, (9 1/2)(1 ft.) = 9 1/2 feet

16. (27')(18')(1/2') = 243 cu.ft. = 9 cu.yds. (1 cu.yd. = 27 cu.ft.)

17. 2 3/4" ÷ 1/4" = 11/4 . 4/1 = 11

18. Material cost = (300)($.50) = $150. Labor cost = ($7.50)(300/5) = $450. Overhead = (.40)($150+$450) = $240. Profit = .10($150+$450+$240) = $84. Submitted price = $150 + $450 + $240 + $84 = $924

19. 6 = .57735" ÷ 8 = .0722"

20. 127 cm = 1270 mm = 1270/25.4" ≈ 50" = 4.2"

21. (25)(4.5') = 112.5' Then, (112.5X3) = 337.5 lbs.

22. (2")(2")(90") = 360 cu.in. Then, (360)(30) = 108 lbs.

23. (36')(9')(1 1/2') = 486 cu.ft. = 18 cu.yds. (1 cu.yd. = 27 cu.ft.)

24. 4 1/4" ÷ 1/2" = 17/4 . 2/1 = 8 1/2. Then, (8 1/2)(1 ft.) = 8 1/2 ft.

25. (12')(3') = 36 sq.ft. Then, (36)(60) = 2160 lbs.

TEST 3

DIRECTIONS: Each question or incomplete statement is followed by several suggested answers or completions. Select the one that BEST answers the question or completes the statement. *PRINT THE LETTER OF THE CORRECT ANSWER IN THE SPACE AT THE RIGHT.*

1. A right triangular metal sheet for a roofing job has sides of 36 inches and 4 feet. The length of the remaining side is

    A. 7 feet
    B. 6 feet
    C. 60 inches
    D. 90 inches

    1.____

2. A U.S. Standard Gauge thickness is given as 0.15625. This thickness, in fractions of an inch, is MOST NEARLY _____ inches.

    A. 1/8 B. 4/32 C. 5/32 D. 3/64

    2.____

3. The weight per 100 of sheet metal fasteners is given as 2/3 pound. The APPROXIMATE number of fasteners in a 2-pound package is

    A. 166 B. 200 C. 300 D. 266

    3.____

4. The decimal equivalent of 27/32 is MOST NEARLY

    A. 0.813 B. 0.828 C. 0.844 D. 0.859

    4.____

5. If a scaled measurement of 1'3" on the drawing of a sheet metal layout represents an actual length of 10"0", then the drawing has been made to a scale of _____ inch to the foot.

    A. 3/4 B. 1 1/4 C. 1 1/2 D. 1 3/4

    5.____

6. Two and two-thirds tees can be made from one sheet of steel. If 24 tees must be made, then the number of sheets required is

    A. 6 B. 7 C. 8 D. 9

    6.____

7. A main duct 20 inches in diameter discharges into two branch ducts. The sum of the areas of the branches is to be equal to the area of the main duct. One branch is 12 inches in diameter. The diameter of the other branch is _____ inches.

    A. 16 B. 12 C. 10 D. 8

    7.____

8. If steel weighs 480 lbs. per cubic foot, the weight of 10 sheets, each 6 feet by 3 feet by 1/32 inch, is _____ lbs.

    A. 2,700 B. 1,237 C. 270 D. 225

    8.____

9. The area, in square inches, of a right triangle that has sides of 12 1/2, 10, and 7 1/2 inches is

    A. 18 1/4 B. 37 1/2 C. 75 D. 60

    9.____

90

10. In making a container to hold 1 gallon (231 cu.in.) and to be 6 inches in diameter at the top and 8 inches in diameter at the bottom, the height must be, in inches,

    A. 10.0   B. 8.2   C. 4.6   D. 6

11. A sheet metal worker is given a job to make a transition piece from a 8 1/2" diameter duct to an 11 1/4" diameter duct. If the length of the transition piece is 5 1/2" for each inch change in diameter, then the length of the transition piece is

    A. 14 7/8"   B. 15"   C. 15 1/8"   D. 15 1/4"

12. A duct layout is drawn to a scale of 3/8" to a foot. If the length of a run shown on the drawing scales 7 1/2", then the ACTUAL length of the run is

    A. 19'6"   B. 19'9"   C. 20'0"   D. 20'3"

13. An 18" x 24" duct is to be connected to a 24" x 24" duct by means of an eccentric transition piece (3 sides flush). If the taper is to be 1" in 4", then the length of the transition piece is

    A. 6"   B. 12"   C. 18"   D. 24"

14. Twenty-seven pairs of 3/8" diameter rods each 3'3 1/2" long are needed to support a duct.
    If the available rods are ten feet long, then the MINIMUM number of rods that will be needed to make the twenty-seven sets is

    A. 9   B. 12   C. 15   D. 18

15. A rectangular sheet metal air duct with open ends is 12 feet long and 15" x 20" in cross-section. If one square foot of the sheet metal weighs 1/2 pound, then the TOTAL weight of the duct is _____ lbs.

    A. 10   B. 17 1/2   C. 35   D. 150

16. The sum of 1/12 and 1/4 is

    A. 1/3   B. 5/12   C. 7/12   D. 3/8

17. The product of 12 and 2 1/3 is

    A. 27   B. 28   C. 29   D. 30

18. If 4 1/2 is subtracted from 7 1/5, the remainder is

    A. 3 7/10   B. 2 7/10   C. 3 3/10   D. 2 3/10

19. The number of cubic yards in 47 cubic feet is MOST NEARLY

    A. 1.70   B. 1.74   C. 1.78   D. 1.82

20. A wall 8'0" high by 12'6" long has a window opening 4'0" high by 3'6" wide. The net area of the wall (allowing for the window opening) is, in square feet,

    A. 86   B. 87   C. 88   D. 89

21. A worker's hourly rate is $11.36. 21.____
    If he works 11 1/2 hours, he should receive

    A. $129.84   B. $130.64   C. $131.48   D. $132.24

22. The number of cubic feet in 3 cubic yards is 22.____

    A. 81   B. 82   C. 83   D. 84

23. At an annual rate of $.40 per $100, what is the fire insurance premium for one year on a 23.____
    house that is insured for $80,000?

    A. $120   B. $160   C. $240   D. $320

24. A meter equals approximately 1.09 yards. 24.____
    How much longer, in yards, is a 100-meter dash than a 100-yard dash?

    A. 6   B. 8   C. 9   D. 12

25. A train leaves New York City at 8:10 A.M. and arrives in Buffalo at 4:45 P.M. on the same 25.____
    day. How long, in hours and minutes, does it take the train to make the trip?
    _____ hours, _____ minutes.

    A. 6; 22   B. 7; 16   C. 7; 28   D. 8; 35

KEY (CORRECT ANSWERS)

1. C   11. C
2. C   12. C
3. C   13. D
4. C   14. D
5. C   15. C

6. D   16. A
7. A   17. B
8. D   18. B
9. B   19. B
10. D 20. A

21. B
22. A
23. D
24. C
25. D

SOLUTIONS TO PROBLEMS

1. Let x = remaining side. Converting to inches, $x^2 = 36^2 + 48^2$ So, $x^2 = 3600$. Solving, x = 60 inches.

2. $.15625 = \dfrac{15,625}{100,000} = \dfrac{5}{32}$

3. 2 ÷ 2/3 = 3. Then, (3)(100) = 300 fasteners

4. 27/32 = .84375 ≈ .844

5. 1'3" ÷ 10 = 15" ÷ 10 = 1 1/2"

6. 24 ÷ 2 2/3 = 24/1.3/8 = 9

7. Area of main duct = $(\pi)(10^2) = 100\pi$. One of the branches has an area of $(\pi)(6^2) = 36\pi$. Thus, the area of the 2nd branch = $100\pi - 36\pi = 64\pi$. The 2nd branch's radius must be 8" and its diameter must be 16".

8. Volume = (1/384')(6')(3') = .046875 cu.ft. Then, 10 sheets have a volume of .46875 cu.ft. Now, (.46875)(480) = 225 lbs.

9. Note that $(7\ 1/2)^2 + (10)^2 = (12\ 1/2)^2$, so that this is a right triangle. Area = (1/2)(10")(7 1/2") = 37 1/2 sq.in.

10. $231 = \dfrac{h}{3}[(\pi)(3)^2 + (\pi)(4)^2 + \sqrt{(9\pi)(16\pi)}]$, where h = required height. Then,

    $231 = \dfrac{h}{3}(9\pi + 16\pi + 12\pi)$. Simplifying, $231 = 37\pi h/3$.
    Solving, h ~ 5.96" or 6"

11. 11 1/4 - 8 1/2 = 2 3/4. Then, (2 3/4)(5 1/2) = 11/4 . 11/2 = 15 1/8

12. 7 1/2" ÷ 3/8" = 15/2 . 8/3 = 20 Then, (20)(1 ft.) = 20 feet

13. 24" - 18" = 6" Then, (6")(4) = 24"

14. 3'3 1/2" = 39.5". Now, (27)(2)(39.5") = 2133". 10 ft. = 120".
    Finally, 2133 ÷ 120 = 17.775, so 18 rods are needed.

15. Surface area = (2)(12')(1 1/4') + (2)(12')(1 2/3') = 70 sq.ft.
    Then, (70)(1/2 lb.) - 35 lbs.

16. 1/12 + 1/4 = 4/12 = 1/3

17. (12)(2 1/3) = 12/1 . 7/3 = 28

18. 7 1/5 - 4 1/2 = 7 2/10 - 4 5/10 = 6 12/10 - 4 5/10 = 2 7/10

19. 47 cu.ft. = 47/27 cu.yds. = 1.74 cu.yds.

20. (8')(12.5') - (4')(3.5') = 86 sq.ft.

21. ($11.36)(11.5) = $130.64

22. 1 cu.yd. = 27 cu.ft., so 3 cu.yds. = 81 cu.ft.

23. $80,000 ÷ $100 = 800. Then, (800)($.40) = $320

24. 100 meters = 109 yds. Then, 109 - 100 = 9 yds.

25. 4:45 P.M. - 8:10 AM. = 8 hrs. 35 min.

READING COMPREHENSION
UNDERSTANDING AND INTERPRETING WRITTEN MATERIAL
EXAMINATION SECTION
TEST 1

DIRECTIONS: Each question or incomplete statement is followed by several suggested answers or completions. Select the one that BEST answers the question or completes the statement. *PRINT THE LETTER OF THE CORRECT ANSWER IN THE SPACE AT THE RIGHT.*

Questions 1-2.

DIRECTIONS: Questions 1 and 2 are to be answered SOLELY on the basis of the following paragraph.

When fixing an upper sash cord, you must also remove the lower sash. To do this, the parting strip between the sash must be removed. Now remove the cover from the weight box channel, cut off the cord as before, and pull it over the pulleys. Pull your new cord over the pulleys and down into the channel where it may be fastened to the weight. The cord for an upper sash is cut off 1" or 2" below the pulley with the weight resting on the floor of the pocket and the cord held taut. These measurements allow for slight stretching of the cord. When the cord is cut to length, it can be pulled up over the pulley and tied with a single common knot in the end to fit into the socket in the sash groove. If the knot protrudes beyond the face of the sash, tap it gently to flatten. In this way, it will not become frayed from constant rubbing against the groove.

1. When repairing the upper sash cord, the FIRST thing to do is to
    A. remove the lower sash
    B. cut the existing sash cord
    C. remove the parting strip
    D. measure the length of new cord necessary

1._____

2. According to the above paragraph, the rope may become frayed if the
    A. pulley is too small   B. knot sticks out
    C. cord is too long   D. weight is too heavy

2._____

Questions 3-4.

DIRECTIONS: Questions 3 and 4 are to be answered SOLELY on the basis of the following paragraph.

Repeated burning of the same area should be avoided. Burning should not be done on impervious, shallow, unstable, or highly erodible soils, or on steep slopes— especially in areas subject to heavy rains or rapid snowmelt. When existing vegetation is likely to be killed or seriously weakened by the fire, measures should be taken to assure prompt revegetation of the burned area. Burns should be limited to relatively small proportions of a watershed unit so that the stream channels will be able to carry any increased flows with a minimum of damage.

3. According to the above paragraph, planned burning should be limited to small areas of the watershed because
    - A. the fire can be better controlled
    - B. existing vegetation will be less likely to be killed
    - C. plants will grow quicker in small areas
    - D. there will be less likelihood of damaging floods

4. According to the above paragraph, burning USUALLY should be done on soils that
    - A. readily absorb moisture
    - B. have been burnt before
    - C. exist as a thin layer over rock
    - D. can be flooded by nearby streams

Questions 5-11.

DIRECTIONS: Questions 5 through 11 are to be answered SOLELY on the basis of the following paragraph.

FUSE INFORMATION

Badly bent or distorted fuse clips cannot be permitted. Sometimes, the distortion or bending is so slight that it escapes notice, yet it may be the cause for fuse failures through the heat that is developed by the poor contact. Occasionally, the proper spring tension of the fuse clips has been destroyed by overheating from loose wire connections to the clips. Proper contact surfaces must be maintained to avoid faulty operation of the fuse. Maintenance men should remove oxides that form on the copper and brass contacts, check the clip pressure, and make sure that contact surfaces are not deformed or bent in any way. When removing oxides, use a well-worn file and remove only the oxide film. Do not use sandpaper or emery cloth as hard particles may come off and become embedded in the contact surfaces. All wire connections to the fuse holders should be carefully inspected to see that they are tight.

5. Fuse failure because of poor clip contact or loose connections is due to the resulting
    - A. excessive voltage
    - B. increased current
    - C. lowered resistance
    - D. heating effect

6. Oxides should be removed from fuse contacts by using
    - A. a dull file
    - B. emery cloth
    - C. fine sandpaper
    - D. a sharp file

7. One result of loose wire connections at the terminal of a fuse clip is stated in the above paragraph to be
    - A. loss of tension in the wire
    - B. welding of the fuse to the clip
    - C. distortion of the clip
    - D. loss of tension of the clip

8. Simple reasoning will show that the oxide film referred to is undesirable CHIEFLY because it
   A. looks dull
   B. makes removal of the fuse difficult
   C. weakens the clips
   D. introduces undesirable resistance

9. Fuse clips that are bent very slightly
   A. should be replaced with new clips
   B. should be carefully filed
   C. may result in blowing of the fuse
   D. may prevent the fuse from blowing

10. From the fuse information paragraph, it would be reasonable to conclude that fuse clips
    A. are difficult to maintain
    B. must be given proper maintenance
    C. require more attention than other electrical equipment
    D. are unreliable

11. A safe practical way of checking the tightness of the wire connection to the fuse clips of a live 120-volt lighting circuit is to
    A. feel the connection with your hand to see if it is warm
    B. try tightening with an insulated screwdriver or socket wrench
    C. see if the circuit works
    D. measure the resistance with an ohmmeter

Questions 12-13.

DIRECTIONS: Questions 12 through 13 are to be answered SOLELY on the basis of the following paragraph.

For cast iron pipe lines, the middle ring or sleeve shall have *beveled* ends and shall be high quality cast iron. The middle ring shall have a minimum wall thickness of 3/8" for pipe up to 8", 7/16" for pipe 10" to 30", and 1/2" for pipe over 30", nominal diameter. Minimum length of middle ring shall be 5" for pipe up to 10", 6" for pipe 10" to 30", and 10" for pipe 30" nominal diameter and larger. The middle ring shall not have a center pipe stop, unless otherwise specified.

12. As used in the above paragraph, the word *beveled* means MOST NEARLY
    A. straight   B. slanted   C. curved   D. rounded

13. In accordance with the above paragraph, the middle ring of a 24" nominal diameter pipe would have a minimum wall thickness and length of _____ thick and _____ long.
    A. 3/8"; 5:
    B. 3/8"; 6"
    C. 7/16"; 6"
    D. 1/2"; 6"

Questions 14-17.

DIRECTIONS: Questions 14 through 17 are to be answered SOLELY on the basis of the following paragraph.

Operators spotting loads with long booms and working around men need the smooth, easy operation and positive control of uniform pressure swing clutches. There are no jerks or grabs with these large disc-type clutches because there is always even pressure over the entire clutch lining surface. In the conventional band-type swing clutch, the pressure varies between dead and live ends of the band. The uniform pressure swing clutch has excellent provision for heat dissipation. The driving elements, which are always rotating, have a great number of fins cast in them. This gives them an impeller or blower action for cooling, resulting in longer life and freedom from frequent adjustment.

14. According to the above paragraph, it may be said that conventional band-type swing clutches have
    A. even pressure on the clutch lining
    B. larger contact area
    C. smaller contact area
    D. uneven pressure on the clutch lining

15. According to the above paragraph, machines equipped with uniform pressure swing clutches will
    A. give better service under all conditions
    B. require no clutch adjustment
    C. give positive control of hoist
    D. provide better control of swing

16. According to the above paragraph, it may be said that the rotation of the driving elements of the uniform pressure swing clutch is ALWAYS
    A. continuous   B. constant
    C. varying   D. uncertain

17. According to the above paragraph, freedom from frequent adjustment is due to the
    A. operator's smooth, easy operation
    B. positive control of the clutch
    C. cooling effect of the rotating fins
    D. larger contact area of the bigger clutch

Questions 18-22.

DIRECTIONS: Questions 18 through 22 are to be answered SOLELY on the basis of the following paragraphs.

Exhaust valve clearance adjustment on diesel engines is very important for proper operation of the engine. Insufficient clearance between the exhaust valve stem and the rocker arm causes a loss of compression and, after a while, burning of the valves and valve seat inserts. On the other hand, too much valve clearance will result in noisy operation of the engine.

Exhaust valves that are maintained in good operating condition will result in efficient combustion in the engine. Valve seats must be true and unpitted, and valve stems must work smoothly within the valve guides. Long valve life will result from proper maintenance and operation of the engine.

Engine operating temperatures should be maintained between 160°F and 185°F. Low operating temperatures result in incomplete combustion and the deposit of fuel lacquers on valves.

18. According to the above paragraphs, too much valve clearance will cause the engine to operate
    A. slowly   B. noisily   C. smoothly   D. cold

19. On the basis of the information given in the above paragraphs, operating temperatures of a diesel engine should be between
    A. 125°F and 130°F   B. 140°F and 150°F
    C. 160°F and 185°F   D. 190°F and 205°F

20. According to the above paragraphs, the deposit of fuel lacquers on valves is caused by
    A. high operating temperatures
    B. insufficient valve clearance
    C. low operating temperatures
    D. efficient combustion

21. According to the above paragraphs, for efficient operation of the engine, valve seats must
    A. have sufficient clearance
    B. be true and unpitted
    C. operate at low temperatures
    D. be adjusted regularly

22. According to the above paragraphs, a loss of compression is due to insufficient clearance between the exhaust valve stem and the
    A. rocker arm   B. valve seat
    C. valve seat inserts   D. valve guides

Questions 23-25.

DIRECTIONS: Questions 23 through 25 are to be answered SOLELY on the basis of the following excerpt:

A SPECIFICATION FOR ELECTRIC WORK FOR THE CITY

Breakers shall be equipped with magnetic blowout coils...Handles of breakers shall be trip-free...Breakers shall be designed to carry 100% of trip rating continuously; to have inverse time delay tripping above 100% of trip rating...

23. According to the above paragraph, the breaker shall have provision for
    A. resetting   B. arc quenching
    C. adjusting trip time D. adjusting trip rating

24. According to the above paragraph, the breaker
    A. shall trip easily at exactly 100% of trip rating
    B. shall trip instantly at a little more than 100% of trip rating
    C. should be constructed so that it shall not be possible to prevent it from opening on overload or short circuit by holding the handle in the ON position
    D. shall not trip prematurely at 100% of trip rating

25. According to the above paragraph, the breaker shall trip
   A. instantaneously as soon as 100% of trip rating is reached
   B. instantaneously as soon as 100% of trip rating is exceeded
   C. more quickly the greater the current, once 100% of trip rating is exceeded
   D. after a predetermined fixed time lapse, once 100% of trip rating is reached

25._____

KEY (CORRECT ANSWERS)

1.	C	11.	B
2.	B	12.	B
3.	D	13.	C
4.	A	14.	D
5.	D	15.	D
6.	A	16.	A
7.	D	17.	C
8.	D	18.	B
9.	C	19.	C
10.	B	20.	C

21.	B
22.	A
23.	B
24.	C
25.	C

TEST 2

DIRECTIONS: Each question or incomplete statement is followed by several suggested answers or completions. Select the one that BEST answers the question or completes the statement. *PRINT THE LETTER OF THE CORRECT ANSWER IN THE SPACE AT THE RIGHT.*

Questions 1-4.

DIRECTIONS: Questions 1 through 4 are to be answered SOLELY on the basis of the following paragraph.

A low pressure hot water boiler shall include a relief valve or valves of a capacity such that with the heat generating equipment operating at maximum, the pressure cannot rise more than 20 percent above the maximum allowable working pressure (set pressure) if that is 30 p.s.i. gage or less, nor more than 10 percent if it is more than 30 p.s.i. gage. The difference between the set pressure and the pressure at which the valve is relieving is known as *over-pressure or accumulation.* If the steam relieving capacity in pounds per hour is calculated, it shall be determined by dividing by 1,000 the maximum BTU output at the boiler nozzle obtainable from the heat generating equipment, or by multiplying the square feet of heating surface by five.

1. In accordance with the above paragraph, the capacity of a relief valve should be computed on the basis of
    A. size of boiler
    B. maximum rated capacity of generating equipment
    C. average output of the generating equipment
    D. minimum capacity of generating equipment

1._____

2. In accordance with the above paragraph, with a set pressure of 30 p.s.i. gage, the overpressure should not be more than _____ p.s.i.
    A. 3   B. 6   C. 33   D. 36

2._____

3. In accordance with the above paragraph, a relief valve should start relieving at a pressure equal to the
    A. set pressure
    B. over pressure
    C. over pressure minus set pressure
    D. set pressure plus over pressure

3._____

4. In accordance with the above paragraph, the steam relieving capacity can be computed by
    A. *multiplying* the maximum BTU output by 5
    B. *dividing* the pounds of steam per hour by 1,000
    C. *dividing* the maximum BTU output by the square feet of heating surface
    D. *dividing* the maximum BTU output by 1,000

4._____

Questions 5-8.

DIRECTIONS: Questions 5 through 8 are to be answered SOLELY on the basis of the following paragraph.

Air conditioning units requiring a minimum rate of flow of water in excess of one-half (1/2) gallon per minute shall be metered. Air conditioning equipment with a refrigeration unit which has a definite rate of capacity in tons or fractions thereof, the charge will be at the rate of $30 per annum per ton capacity from the date installed to the date when the supply is metered. Such units, when equipped with an approved water-conserving device, shall be charged at the rate of $4.50 per annum per ton capacity from the date installed to the date when the supply is metered.

5. A man who was in the market for air conditioning equipment was considering three different units. Unit 1 required a flow of 28 gallons of water per hour; Unit 2 required 30 gallons of water per hour; Unit 3 required 32 gallons of water per hour. The man asked the salesman which units would require the installation of a water meter. According to the above passage, the salesman SHOULD answer:
    A. All three units require meters
    B. Units 2 and 3 require meters
    C. Unit 3 only requires a meter
    D. None of the units require a meter

6. Suppose that air conditioning equipment with a refrigeration unit of 10 tons was put in operation on October 1; and in the following year on July 1, a meter was installed. According to the above passage, the charge for this period would be _____ the annual rate.
    A. twice   B. equal to
    C. three-fourths   D. one-fourth

7. The charge for air conditioning equipment which has no refrigeration unit
    A. is $30 per year
    B. is $25.50 per year
    C. is $4.50 per year
    D. cannot be determined from the above passage

8. The charge for air conditioning equipment with a seven-ton refrigeration unit equipped with an approved water-conserving device
    A. is $4.50 per year
    B. is $25.50 per year
    C. is $31.50 per year
    D. cannot be determined from the above passage

Questions 9-14.

DIRECTIONS: Questions 9 through 14 are to be answered SOLELY on the basis of the following paragraph.

The city makes unremitting efforts to keep the water free from pollution. An inspectional force under a sanitary expert is engaged in patrolling the watersheds to see that the department's sanitary regulations are observed. Samples taken daily from various points in the water supply system are examined and analyzed at the three laboratories maintained by the department. All water before delivery to the distribution mains is treated with chlorine to destroy bacteria. In addition, some water is aerated to free it from gases and, in some cases, from microscopic organisms. Generally, microscopic organisms which develop in the reservoirs and at times impart an unpleasant taste and odor to the water, though in no sense harmful to health, are destroyed by treatment with copper sulfate and by chlorine dosage. None of the supplies is filtered, but the quality of the water supplied by the city is excellent for all purposes, and it is clear and wholesome.

9. According to the above paragraph, microscopic organisms are removed from the water supplied to the city by means of
   A. chlorine alone
   B. chlorine, aeration, and filtration
   C. chlorine, aeration, filtration, and sampling
   D. copper sulfate, chlorine, and aeration

10. Microscopic organisms in the water supply GENERALLY are
    A. a health menace
    B. impossible to detect
    C. not harmful to health
    D. not destroyed in the water

11. The MAIN function of the inspectional force, as described in the above paragraph, is to
    A. take samples of water for analysis
    B. enforce sanitary regulations
    C. add chlorine to the water supply
    D. inspect water-use meters

12. According to the above paragraph, chlorine is added to water before entering the
    A. watersheds
    B. reservoirs
    C. distribution mains
    D. run-off areas

13. Of the following suggested headings or titles for the above paragraph, the one that BEST tells what the paragraph is about is
    A. QUALITY OF WATER
    B. CHLORINATION OF WATER
    C. TESTING OF WATER
    D. BACTERIA IN WATER

14. The MOST likely reason for taking samples of water for examination and analysis from various points in the water supply system is:
    A. The testing points are convenient to the department's laboratories
    B. Water from one part of the system may be made undrinkable by a local condition
    C. The samples can be distributed equally among the three laboratories
    D. The hardness or softness of water varies from place to place

Questions 15-17.

DIRECTIONS: Questions 15 through 17 are to be answered SOLELY on the basis of the following paragraph.

A building measuring 200' x 100' at the street is set back 20' on all sides at the 15th floor, and an additional 10' on all sides at the 30th floor. The building is 35 stories high.

15. The floor area of the 16th floor is MOST NEARLY _____ sq. ft.
    A. 20,000   B. 14,400   C. 9,600   D. 7,500

16. The floor area of the 35th floor is MOST NEARLY _____ sq. ft.
    A. 20,000   B. 13,900   C. 7,500   D. 5,600

17. The floor area of the 16th floor, compared to the floor area of the 2nd floor, is MOST NEARLY _____ as much.
    A. three-fourths (3/4)
    B. two-thirds (2/3)
    C. one-half (1/2)
    D. four-tenths (4/10)

Question 18.

DIRECTIONS: Question 18 is to be answered SOLELY on the basis of the following paragraph.

Experience has shown that, in general, a result of the installation of meters on services not previously metered is to reduce the amount of water consumed, but is not necessarily to reduce the peak load on plumbing systems. The permissible head loss through meters at their rated maximum flow is 20 p.s.i. The installation of a meter may therefore appreciably lower the pressures available in fixtures on a plumbing system.

18. According to the above paragraph, a water meter may
    A. limit the flow in the plumbing system of 20 p.s.i.
    B. reduce the peak load on the plumbing system
    C. increase the overall amount of water consumed
    D. reduce the pressure in the plumbing system

Question 19.

DIRECTIONS: Question 19 is to be answered SOLELY on the basis of the following paragraph.

Spring comes without trumpets to a city. The asphalt is a wilderness that does not quicken overnight; winds blow gritty with cinders instead of merry with the smells of earth and fertilizer. Women wear their gardens on their hats. But spring is a season in the city, and it has its own harbingers, constant as daffodils. Shop windows change their colors, people walk more slowly on the streets, what one can see of the sky has a bluer tone. Pulitzer prizes awake and sing and matinee tickets go-a-begging. But gayer than any of these are the carousels, which are already in sheltered places, beginning to turn with the sound of springtime itself. They are the earliest and the truest and the oldest of all the urban signs.

19. In the passage above, the word *harbingers* means
    A. storms   B. truths   C. virtues   D. forerunners

Questions 20-22.

DIRECTIONS: Questions 20 through 22 are to be answered SOLELY on the basis of the following paragraph.

Gas heaters include manually operated, automatic, and instantaneous heaters. Some heaters are equipped with a thermostat which controls the fuel supply so that when the water falls below a predetermined temperature, the fuel is automatically turned on. In some types, the hot-water storage tank is well-insulated to economize the use of fuel. Instantaneous heaters are arranged so that the opening of a faucet on the hot-water pipe will increase the flow of fuel, which is ignited by a continuously burning pilot light to heat the water to from 120° to 130°F. The possibility that the pilot light will die out offers a source of danger in the use of automatic appliances which depend on a pilot light. Gas and oil heaters are dangerous, and they should be designed to prevent the accumulation, in a confined space within the heater, of a large volume of an explosive mixture.

20. According to the above passage, the opening of a hot-water faucet on a hot-water pipe connected to an instantaneous hot-water heater will the pilot light.
    A. *increase* the temperature of
    B. *increase* the flow of fuel to
    C. *decrease* the flow of fuel to
    D. *have a marked effect* on

21. According to the above passage, the fuel is automatically turned on in a heater equipped with a thermostat whenever
    A. the water temperature drops below 120°F
    B. the pilot light is lit
    C. the water temperature drops below some predetermined temperature
    D. a hot water supply is opened

22. According to the above passage, some hot-water storage tanks are well-insulated to
    A. accelerate the burning of the fuel
    B. maintain the water temperature between 120° and 130°F
    C. prevent the pilot light from being extinguished
    D. minimize the expenditure of fuel

Question 23.

DIRECTIONS: Question 23 is to be answered SOLELY on the basis of the following paragraph.

Breakage of the piston under high-speed operation has been the commonest fault of disc piston meters. Various techniques are adopted to prevent this, such as *throttling* the meter, cutting away the edge of the piston, or reinforcing it, but these are simply makeshifts.

23. As used in the above paragraph, the word *throttling* means MOST NEARLY
    A. enlarging   B. choking
    C. harnessing   D. dismantling

Questions 24-25.

DIRECTIONS: Questions 24 and 25 are to be answered SOLELY on the basis of the following paragraph.

One of the most common and objectionable difficulties occurring in a drainage system is trap seal loss. This failure can be attributed directly to inadequate ventilation of the trap and the subsequent negative and positive pressures which occur. A trap seal may be lost either by siphonage and/or back pressure. Loss of the trap seal by siphonage is the result of a negative pressure in the drainage system. The seal content of the trap is forced by siphonage into the waste piping of the drainage system through exertion of atmospheric pressure on the fixture side of the trap seal.

24. According to the above paragraph, a positive pressure is a direct result of
   A. siphonage
   B. unbalanced trap seal
   C. poor ventilation
   D. atmospheric pressure

25. According to the above paragraph, the water in the trap is forced into the drain pipe by
   A. atmospheric pressure
   B. back pressure
   C. negative pressure
   D. back pressure on fixture side of seal

KEY (CORRECT ANSWERS)

1.	B	11.	B
2.	B	12.	C
3.	D	13.	A
4.	D	14.	B
5.	C	15.	C
6.	C	16.	D
7.	D	17.	C
8.	C	18.	D
9.	D	19.	B
10.	C	20.	B

21.	C
22.	D
23.	B
24.	C
25.	A

www.ingramcontent.com/pod-product-compliance
Lightning Source LLC
Chambersburg PA
CBHW082212300426
44117CB00016B/2772